THE DAILY READING BIBLE

Volume 4

MATTHEW 8-16   NEHEMIAH   HEBREWS 8-13

The Daily Reading Bible (Volume 4)
© Matthias Media 2005

Matthias Media
(St Matthias Press Ltd ACN 067 558 365)
PO Box 225
Kingsford NSW 2032
Australia
Ph: (02) 9663 1478; Int. +61-2-9663-1478
Fax: (02) 9663 3265; Int. +61-2-9663-3265
Email: info@matthiasmedia.com.au
Internet: www.matthiasmedia.com.au

Matthias Media (USA)
Ph: 724 964 8152; Int. +1-724-964-8152
Fax: 724 964 8166; Int. +1-724-964-8166
Email: sales@matthiasmedia.com
Internet: www.matthiasmedia.com

ISBN 978 1 921068 06 5

Cover design and typesetting: www.madebydesign.com.au

CONTENTS

INTRODUCTION

Reading our Bibles regularly is getting harder. That, at least, seems to be the common experience of many Christians. We could waste lots of ink speculating on the reasons for this: is it the frenetic pace of life these days? Is it spiritual laziness? Is it the impact of postmodernism on our culture and the lack of certainty when it comes to interpreting the written word?

But a better option than speculating on the reasons, we thought, was to provide a new resource for Christians to help them get back into a more regular habit of reflecting daily on God's Word. So back in June 2001, we decided to start including a section called 'Bible Brief' in our monthly magazine, *The Briefing* (see www.matthiasmedia.com.au for more information about *The Briefing*). The 'Bible Brief' provided 20 short readings each month—acknowledging that there will be days we miss or days when we want to do something a bit different—with questions, thoughts to ponder, and suggestions to get started in prayer.

Now, some four years later, we have a good collection of 'Bible Briefs', and it's time to offer them to a wider audience in a format that will, we hope, be even more convenient and useful.

This fourth volume contains 60 readings, all designed to be done in 15-20 minutes. These short daily Bible readings are designed to help you feed regularly from God's word. They won't cover every issue in each passage, nor even every passage from each Bible book. In other words, *they are no substitute for the in-depth study of the Scriptures* that you may undertake personally, in small groups or through listening to sermons.

With the kind permission of our friends at Crossway Bibles, we've been able to make this a complete package to take with you—we've included the English Standard Version Bible text with each daily study. So you can take this one book with you and have everything you need—on the train, on the bus, or to the park at lunchtime—wherever and whenever you can get 20 minutes to yourself.

How to use these readings

- *With a penitent heart,* the true prerequisite for all Bible reading. Open with prayer (perhaps using the prayer suggested at the beginning of each set of studies).
- *With 15-20 minutes* of peace and quiet. If you can take longer, and want to read and pray further—great! But we have designed the readings to be done in a fairly short space of time.
- *With an accurate modern translation.* We recommend and have included the new ESV translation. The writers of the studies refer to this translation. Contact us for further details about the ESV or visit www.matthiasmedia.com.au/ESV
- *With a pen.* Even if you only jot down brief ideas, writing focuses the mind.

- *As a guide and help, not a straitjacket.* Feel free to dig further into the passage, to notice and ponder things that the questions don't point to.
- *As a launch-pad for prayer.* Use the prayer ideas at the end of each reading as a starting point for your daily prayer. Many of the points that will arise from the readings will be things you can pray for yourself, and also for others (family, friends, neighbours, etc.). Why not compile a list of people you want to pray for (you can write them in the blank space below), and use the prayer ideas from each reading to pray for the next person on your list?

This fourth volume includes:
- studies on Matthew 8-16 (written by Rory Shiner, a staff worker with the Christian Union at the University of Western Australia)
- studies on the book of Nehemiah (written by Phil Campbell, who ministers at Mitchelton Presbyterian Church in Brisbane, and Greg Clarke, Director of the Centre for Apologetic Scholarship and Education at New College, UNSW)
- studies on Hebrews 8-13 (written by Dave Starling, pastor of Petersham Baptist Church and lecturer in New Testament at Morling College in Sydney).

Matthias Media
August 2005

Please note: the main section of Scripture for each study is reproduced before the questions. Other Scripture references are reproduced as footnotes at the bottom of the page, or, where the passages are too long to be included as footnotes, in the appendix.

PEOPLE TO PRAY FOR:

MATTHEW 8-16

INTRODUCTION

Chapters 8-16 of Matthew are classic examples of those familiar (sometimes all too familiar) gospel stories. There are healings, exorcisms, teachings and miracles—all no doubt amazing at the time, and still impressive after the first few readings; however, once you've read them more than a few times they can become, well, familiar.

What happens, though, if you slow down—really slow down—and read these stories closely? You begin to discover things you may never have seen before: the way Matthew has arranged the stories; the way one story fits with another; the perplexing word; the surprising turn; the less-than-familiar parable. This is the challenge for these readings: to read these passages with some care—and who knows? You may just discover some pearls of great price.

Here's an opening prayer you might like to use before each of the next 20 studies:

God my Father,
Thank you for preserving your word for us. Help me today to read familiar words afresh,
difficult words aright, and gracious words with thankfulness.
For Jesus' sake,
Amen.

NB: Tick the box when you've completed each study ✓

READING 1   MATTHEW 7:28-8:4 ☐

And when Jesus finished these sayings, the crowds were astonished at his teaching, ²⁹ for he was teaching them as one who had authority, and not as their scribes.
8:1 When he came down from the mountain, great crowds followed him. ² And behold, a leper came to him and knelt before him, saying, "Lord, if you will, you can make me clean." ³ And Jesus stretched out his hand and touched him, saying, "I will; be clean." And immediately his leprosy was cleansed. ⁴ And Jesus said to him, "See that you say nothing to anyone, but go, show yourself to the priest and offer the gift that Moses commanded, for a proof to them."

1. Jesus has just finished teaching the Sermon on the Mount (Matthew 5-7). What struck the original hearers about Jesus' teaching (7:29)?

2. In these verses (7:28-8:4) what impression do you get of:
a. the crowds?

b. the scribes (NIV "teachers of the law")?

c. the priests?

3. Consider the incident in 8:1-4. According to Levitical law, when a 'clean' person touches an 'unclean' person there are serious consequences, involving isolating the unclearn person for a period of days, followed by washing and ritual sacrifice (cf. Lev 13-14, printed in the appendix on pp. 70-74.) How is Jesus' contact with the unclean different?

PONDER Jesus' relationship with Israel—its law, its leaders, its institutions—is a key theme in Matthew. Keep the question of Jesus' relationship to the institutions of Israel in the back of your mind as you read through Matthew (it may even shed some light on 8:4!). A fruitful exercise would be to write the headings 'scribes', 'crowds', 'Pharisees', etc. on a page, and keep jotting down information as you read, so as to build up a complete picture. We've included space at the end of these studies for you to do this (p. 76).

PRAYER IDEAS Thank God that, in Jesus, cleanness finally trumps uncleanness. Pray that Jesus will 'astonish' you this month.

READING 2   MATTHEW 8:5-34

When he entered Capernaum, a centurion came forward to him, appealing to him, ⁶ "Lord, my servant is lying paralyzed at home, suffering terribly." ⁷ And he said to him, "I will come and heal him." ⁸ But the centurion replied, "Lord, I am not worthy to have you come under my roof, but only say the word, and my servant will be healed. ⁹ For I too am a man under authority, with soldiers under me. And I say to one, 'Go,' and he goes, and to another, 'Come,' and he comes, and to my servant, 'Do this,' and he does it." ¹⁰ When Jesus heard this, he marveled and said to those who followed him, "Truly, I tell you, with no one in Israel have I found such faith. ¹¹ I tell you, many will come from east and west and recline at table with Abraham, Isaac, and Jacob in the kingdom of heaven, ¹² while the sons of the kingdom will be thrown into the outer darkness. In that place there will be weeping and gnashing of teeth." ¹³ And to the centurion Jesus said, "Go; let it be done for you as you have believed." And the servant was healed at that very moment.

¹⁴ And when Jesus entered Peter's house, he saw his mother-in-law lying sick with a fever. ¹⁵ He touched her hand, and the fever left her, and she rose and began to serve him. ¹⁶ That evening they brought to him many who were oppressed by demons, and he cast out the spirits with a word and healed all who were sick. ¹⁷ This was to fulfill what was spoken by the prophet Isaiah: "He took our illnesses and bore our diseases."

¹⁸ Now when Jesus saw a great crowd around him, he gave orders to go over to the other side. ¹⁹ And a scribe came up and said to him, "Teacher, I will follow you wherever you go." ²⁰ And Jesus said to him, "Foxes have holes, and birds of the air have nests, but the Son of Man has nowhere to lay his head." ²¹ Another of the disciples said to him, "Lord, let me first go and bury my father." ²² And Jesus said to him, "Follow me, and leave the dead to bury their own dead."

²³ And when he got into the boat, his disciples followed him. ²⁴ And behold, there arose a great storm on the sea, so that the boat was being swamped by the waves; but he was asleep. ²⁵ And they went and woke him, saying, "Save us, Lord; we are

perishing." 26 And he said to them, "Why are you afraid, O you of little faith?" Then he rose and rebuked the winds and the sea, and there was a great calm. 27 And the men marveled, saying, "What sort of man is this, that even winds and sea obey him?"

28 And when he came to the other side, to the country of the Gadarenes, two demon-possessed men met him, coming out of the tombs, so fierce that no one could pass that way. 29 And behold, they cried out, "What have you to do with us, O Son of God? Have you come here to torment us before the time?" 30 Now a herd of many pigs was feeding at some distance from them. 31 And the demons begged him, saying, "If you cast us out, send us away into the herd of pigs." 32 And he said to them, "Go." So they came out and went into the pigs, and behold, the whole herd rushed down the steep bank into the sea and drowned in the waters. 33 The herdsmen fled, and going into the city they told everything, especially what had happened to the demon-possessed men. 34 And behold, all the city came out to meet Jesus, and when they saw him, they begged him to leave their region.

1. *There are five little incidents recorded in these verses. Go through them, labelling each one as a particular type of story (e.g. 'a healing story'). Then for each story, try and find a one-word summary of what the story is teaching (e.g. 'faith').*

a. *Incident 1*

b. *Incident 2*

c. *Incident 3*

d. *Incident 4*

e. *Incident 5*

2. *We are used to people marvelling (being astonished) at Jesus (NIV "amazed"; e.g. Matt 8:27). What is it here that makes Jesus marvel (8:10)? Why is it such a marvel to him (vv. 10-13)?*

PONDER The demons ask Jesus if he has come to torment them "before the time". Which 'time' do you think they are speaking of?

PRAYER IDEAS "What sort of man is this?" (v. 27). Thank God that he has given us this sort of man—compassionate, healing, powerful and good.

READING 3   **MATTHEW 9:1-8**

And getting into a boat he crossed over and came to his own city. 2 And behold, some people brought to him a paralytic, lying on a bed. And when Jesus saw their faith, he said to the paralytic, "Take heart, my son; your sins are forgiven." 3 And behold, some of the scribes said to themselves, "This man is blaspheming." 4 But Jesus, knowing their thoughts, said, "Why do you think evil in your hearts? 5 For which is easier, to say, 'Your sins are forgiven,' or to say, 'Rise and walk'? 6 But that you may know that the Son of Man has authority on earth to forgive sins"—he then said to the paralytic—"Rise, pick up your bed and go home." 7 And he rose and went home. 8 When the crowds saw it, they were afraid, and they glorified God, who had given such authority to men.

1. Jot down the various reactions of the people in this story. How do/does Jesus, the scribes, and the crowds react to events?

2. Why do people react in the way that they do, i.e. why do you think the scribes perceive blasphemy? Why are the crowds afraid? Why does Jesus forgive, then heal?

3. What do the crowds glorify God on account of (v. 8)? Why do you think it is a reason for glorifying God?

PONDER If you were sharing the gospel with a friend, which gospel points do you think you could demonstrate from these verses?

PRAYER IDEAS Pray that your time spent studying Jesus in these studies will, like the crowds, move you to fear and glorify God.

READING 4 — MATTHEW 9:9-13 (SEE ALSO 12:7)

As Jesus passed on from there, he saw a man called Matthew sitting at the tax booth, and he said to him, "Follow me." And he rose and followed him.
[10] And as Jesus reclined at table in the house, behold, many tax collectors and sinners came and were reclining with Jesus and his disciples. [11] And when the Pharisees saw this, they said to his disciples, "Why does your teacher eat with tax collectors and sinners?" [12] But when he heard it, he said, "Those who are well have no need of a physician, but those who are sick. [13] Go and learn what this means, 'I desire mercy, and not sacrifice.' For I came not to call the righteous, but sinners."

....

12:7 And if you had known what this means, 'I desire mercy, and not sacrifice,' you would not have condemned the guiltless.

1. How would you describe Matthew's reaction to Jesus? (If you are keeping notes about the reactions of various people to Jesus, you may like to add another group at this point—'sinners').

2. What is Jesus accused of? How does Jesus defend himself?

3. What should they have learnt from the verse "I desire mercy and not sacrifice" (Hos 6:6[1])? Noting that Jesus quotes this verse again in 12:7, why do you think Jesus thought this text was so important?

PONDER If people were observing your hospitality and social patterns—who you eat with, whose company you keep—what might they be able to accuse you of?

PRAYER IDEAS Thank God that Jesus has been prepared to keep bad company—with you!

---

1. For I desire steadfast love and not sacrifice, the knowledge of God rather than burnt offerings.

Then the disciples of John came to him, saying, "Why do we and the Pharisees fast, but your disciples do not fast?" 15 And Jesus said to them, "Can the wedding guests mourn as long as the bridegroom is with them? The days will come when the bridegroom is taken away from them, and then they will fast. 16 No one puts a piece of unshrunk cloth on an old garment, for the patch tears away from the garment, and a worse tear is made. 17 Neither is new wine put into old wineskins. If it is, the skins burst and the wine is spilled and the skins are destroyed. But new wine is put into fresh wineskins, and so both are preserved."

18 While he was saying these things to them, behold, a ruler came in and knelt before him, saying, "My daughter has just died, but come and lay your hand on her, and she will live." 19 And Jesus rose and followed him, with his disciples. 20 And behold, a woman who had suffered from a discharge of blood for twelve years came up behind him and touched the fringe of his garment, 21 for she said to herself, "If I only touch his garment, I will be made well." 22 Jesus turned, and seeing her he said, "Take heart, daughter; your faith has made you well." And instantly the woman was made well. 23 And when Jesus came to the ruler's house and saw the flute players and the crowd making a commotion, 24 he said, "Go away, for the girl is not dead but sleeping." And they laughed at him. 25 But when the crowd had been put outside, he went in and took her by the hand, and the girl arose. 26 And the report of this went through all that district.

27 And as Jesus passed on from there, two blind men followed him, crying aloud, "Have mercy on us, Son of David." 28 When he entered the house, the blind men came to him, and Jesus said to them, "Do you believe that I am able to do this?" They said to him, "Yes, Lord." 29 Then he touched their eyes, saying, "According to your faith be it done to you." 30 And their eyes were opened. And Jesus sternly warned them, "See that no one knows about it." 31 But they went away and spread his fame through all that district.

32 As they were going away, behold, a demon-oppressed man who was mute was brought to him. 33 And when the demon had been cast out, the mute man spoke. And the crowds marveled, saying, "Never was anything like this seen in Israel." 34 But the Pharisees said, "He casts out demons by the prince of demons."

35 And Jesus went throughout all the cities and villages, teaching in their synagogues and proclaiming the gospel of the kingdom and healing every disease and every affliction. 36 When he saw the crowds, he had compassion for them, because they were harassed and helpless, like sheep without a shepherd. 37 Then he said to his disciples, "The harvest is plentiful, but the laborers are few; 38 therefore pray earnestly to the Lord of the harvest to send out laborers into his harvest."

1. Matthew 9:14-38 gives you the impression that a lot of things happen in quick succession. Read over the passage again, noting all that happens from Jesus being questioned by John's disciples (v. 14) to the preaching and healing tour (vv. 35-38).

2. There are a number of different 'characters' Jesus encounters in this section (John's disciples, the blind men, the crowds, etc.) Jot down each one, and try to think of an adjective to describe each of their reactions to Jesus (e.g. 'offended').

PONDER What is 'faith' in these verses?

PRAYER IDEAS Pray for those who suffer illness—especially illness which excludes them from society.

READING 6   MATTHEW 10

And he called to him his twelve disciples and gave them authority over unclean spirits, to cast them out, and to heal every disease and every affliction. 2 The names of the twelve apostles are these: first, Simon, who is called Peter, and Andrew his brother; James the son of Zebedee, and John his brother; 3 Philip and Bartholomew; Thomas and Matthew the tax collector; James the son of Alphaeus, and Thaddaeus; 4 Simon the Cananaean, and Judas Iscariot, who betrayed him.

5 These twelve Jesus sent out, instructing them, "Go nowhere among the Gentiles and enter no town of the Samaritans, 6 but go rather to the lost sheep of the house of Israel. 7 And proclaim as you go, saying, 'The kingdom of heaven is at hand.' 8 Heal the sick, raise the dead, cleanse lepers, cast out demons. You received without paying; give without pay. 9 Acquire no gold nor silver nor copper for your belts, 10 no bag for your journey, nor two tunics nor sandals nor a staff, for the laborer deserves his food. 11 And whatever town or village you enter, find out who is worthy in it and stay there until you depart. 12 As you enter the house, greet it. 13 And if the house is worthy, let your peace come upon it, but if it is not worthy, let your peace return to you. 14 And if anyone will not receive you or listen to your words, shake off the dust from your feet when you leave that house or town. 15 Truly, I say to you, it will be more bearable on the day of judgment for the land of Sodom and Gomorrah than

for that town.

16 "Behold, I am sending you out as sheep in the midst of wolves, so be wise as serpents and innocent as doves. 17 Beware of men, for they will deliver you over to courts and flog you in their synagogues, 18 and you will be dragged before governors and kings for my sake, to bear witness before them and the Gentiles. 19 When they deliver you over, do not be anxious how you are to speak or what you are to say, for what you are to say will be given to you in that hour. 20 For it is not you who speak, but the Spirit of your Father speaking through you. 21 Brother will deliver brother over to death, and the father his child, and children will rise against parents and have them put to death, 22 and you will be hated by all for my name's sake. But the one who endures to the end will be saved. 23 When they persecute you in one town, flee to the next, for truly, I say to you, you will not have gone through all the towns of Israel before the Son of Man comes.

24 "A disciple is not above his teacher, nor a servant above his master. 25 It is enough for the disciple to be like his teacher, and the servant like his master. If they have called the master of the house Beelzebul, how much more will they malign those of his household.

26 "So have no fear of them, for nothing is covered that will not be revealed, or hidden that will not be known. 27 What I tell you in the dark, say in the light, and what you hear whispered, proclaim on the housetops. 28 And do not fear those who kill the body but

cannot kill the soul. Rather fear him who can destroy both soul and body in hell. [29] Are not two sparrows sold for a penny? And not one of them will fall to the ground apart from your Father. [30] But even the hairs of your head are all numbered. [31] Fear not, therefore; you are of more value than many sparrows. [32] So everyone who acknowledges me before men, I also will acknowledge before my Father who is in heaven, [33] but whoever denies me before men, I also will deny before my Father who is in heaven.

[34] "Do not think that I have come to bring peace to the earth. I have not come to bring peace, but a sword. [35] For I have come to set a man against his father, and a daughter against her mother, and a daughter-in-law against her mother-in-law. [36] And a person's enemies will be those of his own household. [37] Whoever loves father or mother more than me is not worthy of me, and whoever loves son or daughter more than me is not worthy of me. [38] And whoever does not take his cross and follow me is not worthy of me. [39] Whoever finds his life will lose it, and whoever loses his life for my sake will find it.

[40] "Whoever receives you receives me, and whoever receives me receives him who sent me. [41] The one who receives a prophet because he is a prophet will receive a prophet's reward, and the one who receives a righteous person because he is a righteous person will receive a righteous person's reward. [42] And whoever gives one of these little ones even a cup of cold water because he is a disciple, truly, I say to you, he will by no means lose his reward."

1. Matthew 10 sees Jesus gathering his twelve disciples and sending them out on a mission to Israel (see 9:35-38 on p. 11 for context). Note anything that strikes you as unusual in Jesus' instructions to them.

2. How would you describe the <u>tone</u> of the speech?

3. In one sentence, how would you describe the purpose of this mission?

PONDER What did you notice about Israel and the Gentiles in these verses? Consider Matthew 21:43[2] and 28:19.[3]

PRAYER IDEAS Thank God for those who experienced hardship in getting the message of the kingdom to you.

READING 7   MATTHEW 10

And he called to him his twelve disciples and gave them authority over unclean spirits, to cast them out, and to heal every disease and every affliction. [2] The names of the twelve apostles are these: first, Simon, who is called Peter, and Andrew his brother; James the son of Zebedee, and John his brother; [3] Philip and Bartholomew; Thomas and Matthew the tax collector; James the son of Alphaeus, and Thaddaeus; [4] Simon the Cananaean, and Judas Iscariot, who betrayed him.

[5] These twelve Jesus sent out, instructing them, "Go nowhere among the Gentiles and enter no town of the Samaritans, [6] but go rather to the lost sheep of the house of

---

2. "Therefore I tell you, the kingdom of God will be taken away from you and given to a people producing its fruits."

3. "Go therefore and make disciples of all nations, baptizing them in the name of the Father and of the Son and of the Holy Spirit ..."

Israel. 7 And proclaim as you go, saying, 'The kingdom of heaven is at hand.' 8 Heal the sick, raise the dead, cleanse lepers, cast out demons. You received without paying; give without pay. 9 Acquire no gold nor silver nor copper for your belts, 10 no bag for your journey, nor two tunics nor sandals nor a staff, for the laborer deserves his food. 11 And whatever town or village you enter, find out who is worthy in it and stay there until you depart. 12 As you enter the house, greet it. 13 And if the house is worthy, let your peace come upon it, but if it is not worthy, let your peace return to you. 14 And if anyone will not receive you or listen to your words, shake off the dust from your feet when you leave that house or town. 15 Truly, I say to you, it will be more bearable on the day of judgment for the land of Sodom and Gomorrah than for that town.

16 "Behold, I am sending you out as sheep in the midst of wolves, so be wise as serpents and innocent as doves. 17 Beware of men, for they will deliver you over to courts and flog you in their synagogues, 18 and you will be dragged before governors and kings for my sake, to bear witness before them and the Gentiles. 19 When they deliver you over, do not be anxious how you are to speak or what you are to say, for what you are to say will be given to you in that hour. 20 For it is not you who speak, but the Spirit of your Father speaking through you. 21 Brother will deliver brother over to death, and the father his child, and children will rise against parents and have them put to death, 22 and you will be hated by all for my name's sake. But the one who endures to the end will be saved. 23 When they persecute you in one town, flee to the next, for truly, I say to you, you will not have gone through all the towns of Israel before the Son of Man comes.

24 "A disciple is not above his teacher, nor a servant above his master. 25 It is enough for the disciple to be like his teacher, and the servant like his master. If they have called the master of the house Beelzebul, how much more will they malign those of his household.

26 "So have no fear of them, for nothing is covered that will not be revealed, or hidden that will not be known. 27 What I tell you in the dark, say in the light, and what you hear whispered, proclaim on the housetops. 28 And do not fear those who kill the body but cannot kill the soul. Rather fear him who can destroy both soul and body in hell. 29 Are not two sparrows sold for a penny? And not one of them will fall to the ground apart from your Father. 30 But even the hairs of your head are all numbered. 31 Fear not, therefore; you are of more value than many sparrows. 32 So everyone who acknowledges me before men, I also will acknowledge before my Father who is in heaven, 33 but whoever denies me before men, I also will deny before my Father who is in heaven.

34 "Do not think that I have come to bring peace to the earth. I have not come to bring peace, but a sword. 35 For I have come to set a man against his father, and a daughter against her mother, and a daughter-in-law against her mother-in-law. 36 And a person's enemies will be those of his own household. 37 Whoever loves father or mother more than me is not worthy of me, and whoever loves son or daughter more than me is not worthy of me. 38 And whoever does not take his cross and follow me is not worthy of me. 39 Whoever finds his life will lose it, and whoever loses his life for my sake will find it.

40 "Whoever receives you receives me, and whoever receives me receives him who sent me. 41 The one who receives a prophet because he is a prophet will receive a prophet's reward, and the one who receives a righteous person because he is a righteous person will receive a righteous person's reward. 42 And whoever gives one of these little ones even a cup of cold water because he is a disciple, truly, I say to you, he will by no means lose his reward."

Go through Jesus' speech in Matthew 10 and jot down all that he says under the following headings. What picture of their ministry emerges?

1. Expectations

2. Warnings

3. Encouragements

PONDER Do you think this passage could be used in connection with gospel ministry today? Why or why not?

PRAYER IDEAS Pray for those preaching the gospel in difficult situations today.

READING 8   MATTHEW 11:1-19

When Jesus had finished instructing his twelve disciples, he went on from there to teach and preach in their cities. ² Now when John heard in prison about the deeds of the Christ, he sent word by his disciples ³ and said to him, "Are you the one who is to come, or shall we look for another?" ⁴ And Jesus answered them, "Go and tell John what you hear and see: ⁵ the blind receive their sight and the lame walk, lepers are cleansed and the deaf hear, and the dead are raised up, and the poor have good news preached to them. ⁶ And blessed is the one who is not offended by me."

⁷ As they went away, Jesus began to speak to the crowds concerning John: "What did you go out into the wilderness to see? A reed shaken by the wind? ⁸ What then did you go out to see? A man dressed in soft clothing? Behold, those who wear soft clothing are in kings' houses. ⁹ What then did you go out to see? A prophet? Yes, I tell you, and more than a prophet. ¹⁰ This is he of whom it is written,

"'Behold, I send my messenger before your face,
who will prepare your way before you.'

¹¹ Truly, I say to you, among those born of women there has arisen no one greater than John the Baptist. Yet the one who is least in the kingdom of heaven is greater than he. ¹² From the days of John the Baptist until now the kingdom of heaven has suffered violence,

and the violent take it by force. ¹³ For all the Prophets and the Law prophesied until John, ¹⁴ and if you are willing to accept it, he is Elijah who is to come. ¹⁵ He who has ears to hear, let him hear.

¹⁶ "But to what shall I compare this generation? It is like children sitting in the marketplaces and calling to their playmates,

¹⁷ "'We played the flute for you, and you
did not dance;
we sang a dirge, and you did not mourn.'

¹⁸ For John came neither eating nor drinking, and they say, 'He has a demon.' ¹⁹ The Son of Man came eating and drinking, and they say, 'Look at him! A glutton and a drunkard, a friend of tax collectors and sinners!' Yet wisdom is justified by her deeds."

1. In these verses, the identities of two people, Jesus and John the Baptist, are on view. What is John's question about Jesus' identity? What is Jesus' answer? Is it a 'yes' or a 'no'?

2. What does Jesus confirm about the identity of John?

3. In verses 17-19, what does Jesus say about that generation's reaction to both Jesus and John?

PONDER Jesus' ministry challenged nearly everyone's expectations: the scribes, the crowds—even John the Baptist seems to have been taken by surprise. Why do you think John needed clarification (see 3:11-12[4])?

PRAYER IDEAS Pray for clear teaching about Christ in our generation.

READING 9   MATTHEW 11:20-30

Then he began to denounce the cities where most of his mighty works had been done, because they did not repent. ²¹ "Woe to you, Chorazin! Woe to you, Bethsaida! For if the mighty works done in you had been done in Tyre and Sidon, they would have repented long ago in sackcloth and ashes. ²² But I tell you, it will be more bearable on the day of judgment for Tyre and Sidon than for you. ²³ And you, Capernaum, will you be exalted to heaven? You will be brought down to Hades. For if the mighty works done in you had been done in Sodom, it would have remained until this day. ²⁴ But I tell you that it will be more tolerable on the day of judgment for the land of Sodom than for you."

²⁵ At that time Jesus declared, "I thank you, Father, Lord of heaven and earth, that you have hidden these things from the wise and understanding and revealed them to little children; ²⁶ yes, Father, for such was your gracious will. ²⁷ All things have been handed over to me by my Father, and no one knows the Son except the Father, and no one knows the Father except the Son and anyone to whom the Son chooses to reveal him. ²⁸ Come to me, all who labor and are heavy laden, and I will give you rest. ²⁹ Take my yoke upon you, and learn from me, for I am gentle and lowly in heart, and you will find rest for your souls. ³⁰ For my yoke is easy, and my burden is light."

1. These verses may well be Jesus' reaction to the reports from the mission of chapter 10. If that is right, what seems to have happened?

2. How would you describe the fate of those spoken against in verses 20-24?

3. How would you describe the terms of acceptance laid out by Jesus in verses 25-30?

PONDER If you were teaching about the doctrine of predestination (or just trying to work it out for yourself) how could both 11:25-30 and 11:20-24 flesh out the doctrine?

PRAYER IDEAS Thank God for choosing you.

POINTER Chorazin, Capernaum and Bethsaida are (Jewish) cities in which Jesus (or his disciples) conducted their ministry. Tyre, Sidon and Sodom are all (Gentile) cities mentioned in the Old Testament for their wickedness.

---

4. "I baptize you with water for repentance, but he who is coming after me is mightier than I, whose sandals I am not worthy to carry. He will baptize you with the Holy Spirit and with fire. ¹² His winnowing fork is in his hand, and he will clear his threshing floor and gather his wheat into the barn, but the chaff he will burn with unquenchable fire."

At that time Jesus went through the grainfields on the Sabbath. His disciples were hungry, and they began to pluck heads of grain and to eat. ² But when the Pharisees saw it, they said to him, "Look, your disciples are doing what is not lawful to do on the Sabbath." ³ He said to them, "Have you not read what David did when he was hungry, and those who were with him: ⁴ how he entered the house of God and ate the bread of the Presence, which it was not lawful for him to eat nor for those who were with him, but only for the priests? ⁵ Or have you not read in the Law how on the Sabbath the priests in the temple profane the Sabbath and are guiltless? ⁶ I tell you, something greater than the temple is here. ⁷ And if you had known what this means, 'I desire mercy, and not sacrifice,' you would not have condemned the guiltless. ⁸ For the Son of Man is lord of the Sabbath."

⁹ He went on from there and entered their synagogue. ¹⁰ And a man was there with a withered hand. And they asked him, "Is it lawful to heal on the Sabbath?"—so that they might accuse him. ¹¹ He said to them, "Which one of you who has a sheep, if it falls into a pit on the Sabbath, will not take hold of it and lift it out? ¹² Of how much more value is a man than a sheep! So it is lawful to do good on the Sabbath." ¹³ Then he said to the man, "Stretch out your hand." And the man stretched it out, and it was restored, healthy like the other. ¹⁴ But the Pharisees went out and conspired against him, how to destroy him.

1. What are Jesus and the disciples doing in verses 1-8? What do the Pharisees accuse them of?

2. In both of these stories, Jesus clearly has a different attitude to the Sabbath than the Pharisees. Look through both stories and see what arguments you can find Jesus giving to defend his behaviour.

3. What do you think "something greater than the temple" (v. 6, NIV "one greater than the temple") refers to?

PONDER How do you think these stories might relate to the passage that came before them (11:25-30)?

PRAYER IDEAS Praise God for the Sabbath, the rest, which we have in Christ. Pray that you may know in experience what is true in reality—that you are at rest in him.

Jesus, aware of this, withdrew from there. And many followed him, and he healed them all ¹⁶ and ordered them not to make him known. ¹⁷ This was to fulfill what was spoken by the prophet Isaiah:

¹⁸ "Behold, my servant whom I have chosen,
　my beloved with whom my soul is well pleased.
I will put my Spirit upon him,
　and he will proclaim justice to the Gentiles.
¹⁹ He will not quarrel or cry aloud,
　nor will anyone hear his voice in the streets;
²⁰ a bruised reed he will not break,

MATTHEW 8-16

NEHEMIAH

HEBREWS 8-13

and a smoldering wick he will not
quench,
until he brings justice to victory;
²¹ and in his name the Gentiles will hope."

*1. Why does Jesus withdraw at this point?
(See v. 14 in the previous reading.)*

*2. What does Jesus do that fulfils the
prophecy of Isaiah?*

*3. Why do you think Jesus ordered those
he healed not to make him known (again,
see v. 14)?*

PONDER Read over the quote from Isaiah in
verses 18-21. In what we have been reading
in Matthew, how well does it fit as a
description of Jesus?

PRAYER IDEAS Thank God for the gentleness
of Jesus, and the hope he has won for the
Gentiles. Pray about areas of conflict in the
world where there are bruised reeds and
smoldering wicks, crying out for justice.

READING 12   MATTHEW 12:22-50

Then a demon-oppressed man who was
blind and mute was brought to him, and
he healed him, so that the man spoke and
saw. ²³ And all the people were amazed, and
said, "Can this be the Son of David?" ²⁴ But
when the Pharisees heard it, they said, "It is
only by Beelzebul, the prince of demons, that
this man casts out demons." ²⁵ Knowing their
thoughts, he said to them, "Every kingdom
divided against itself is laid waste, and no
city or house divided against itself will stand.
²⁶ And if Satan casts out Satan, he is divided
against himself. How then will his kingdom
stand? ²⁷ And if I cast out demons by
Beelzebul, by whom do your sons cast them
out? Therefore they will be your judges. ²⁸ But
if it is by the Spirit of God that I cast out
demons, then the kingdom of God has come
upon you. ²⁹ Or how can someone enter a
strong man's house and plunder his goods,
unless he first binds the strong man? Then
indeed he may plunder his house. ³⁰ Whoever
is not with me is against me, and whoever does
not gather with me scatters. ³¹ Therefore I tell
you, every sin and blasphemy will be forgiven
people, but the blasphemy against the Spirit
will not be forgiven. ³² And whoever speaks a
word against the Son of Man will be forgiven,
but whoever speaks against the Holy Spirit
will not be forgiven, either in this age or in
the age to come.

³³ "Either make the tree good and its fruit
good, or make the tree bad and its fruit bad,
for the tree is known by its fruit. ³⁴ You
brood of vipers! How can you speak good,
when you are evil? For out of the abundance
of the heart the mouth speaks. ³⁵ The good
person out of his good treasure brings forth
good, and the evil person out of his evil
treasure brings forth evil. ³⁶ I tell you, on the
day of judgment people will give account for
every careless word they speak, ³⁷ for by your
words you will be justified, and by your
words you will be condemned."

³⁸ Then some of the scribes and Pharisees
answered him, saying, "Teacher, we wish to see
a sign from you." ³⁹ But he answered them,
"An evil and adulterous generation seeks for
a sign, but no sign will be given to it except
the sign of the prophet Jonah. ⁴⁰ For just as
Jonah was three days and three nights in the
belly of the great fish, so will the Son of Man
be three days and three nights in the heart
of the earth. ⁴¹ The men of Nineveh will rise

up at the judgment with this generation and condemn it, for they repented at the preaching of Jonah, and behold, something greater than Jonah is here. ⁴² The queen of the South will rise up at the judgment with this generation and condemn it, for she came from the ends of the earth to hear the wisdom of Solomon, and behold, something greater than Solomon is here.

⁴³ "When the unclean spirit has gone out of a person, it passes through waterless places seeking rest, but finds none. ⁴⁴ Then it says, 'I will return to my house from which I came.' And when it comes, it finds the house empty, swept, and put in order. ⁴⁵ Then it goes and brings with it seven other spirits more evil than itself, and they enter and dwell there, and the last state of that person is worse than the first. So also will it be with this evil generation."

⁴⁶ While he was still speaking to the people, behold, his mother and his brothers stood outside, asking to speak to him.† ⁴⁸ But he replied to the man who told him, "Who is my mother, and who are my brothers?" ⁴⁹ And stretching out his hand toward his disciples, he said, "Here are my mother and my brothers! ⁵⁰ For whoever does the will of my Father in heaven is my brother and sister and mother."

1. In verses 22-32, what are the two theories people have about Jesus' identity? Who holds to which view?

2. What is Jesus' answer to the "prince of demons" accusation?

3. In verses 33-37, Jesus speaks of evil words coming from the mouth. From the context, which evil words do you think he has in mind?

4. Does the context help to make sense of the teaching that speaking "against the Holy Spirit will not be forgiven" (v. 32)?

PONDER What do you think it means to say that "by your words you will be justified, and by your words you will be condemned" (v. 37)?

PRAYER IDEAS Take time to pray for people you love, in light of the coming judgement.

READING 13   MATTHEW 12:22-50 (SEE ALSO 16:1-4)

Then a demon-oppressed man who was blind and mute was brought to him, and he healed him, so that the man spoke and saw. ²³ And all the people were amazed, and said, "Can this be the Son of David?" ²⁴ But when the Pharisees heard it, they said, "It is only by Beelzebul, the prince of demons, that this man casts out demons." ²⁵ Knowing their thoughts, he said to them, "Every kingdom divided against itself is laid waste, and no city or house divided against itself will stand. ²⁶ And if Satan casts out Satan, he is divided against himself. How then will his kingdom stand? ²⁷ And if I cast out demons by Beelzebul, by whom do your sons cast them out? Therefore they will be your judges. ²⁸ But if it is by the Spirit of God that I cast out demons, then the kingdom of God has come upon you. ²⁹ Or how can someone enter a strong man's house and plunder his goods, unless he first binds the strong man? Then indeed he may plunder his house. ³⁰ Whoever is not with me is against me, and whoever does not gather with me scatters. ³¹ Therefore I tell you, every sin and blasphemy will be forgiven people, but the blasphemy against

† Some manuscripts insert verse 47: Someone told him, "Your mother and your brothers are standing outside, asking to speak to you".

the Spirit will not be forgiven. 32 And whoever speaks a word against the Son of Man will be forgiven, but whoever speaks against the Holy Spirit will not be forgiven, either in this age or in the age to come.

33 "Either make the tree good and its fruit good, or make the tree bad and its fruit bad, for the tree is known by its fruit. 34 You brood of vipers! How can you speak good, when you are evil? For out of the abundance of the heart the mouth speaks. 35 The good person out of his good treasure brings forth good, and the evil person out of his evil treasure brings forth evil. 36 I tell you, on the day of judgment people will give account for every careless word they speak, 37 for by your words you will be justified, and by your words you will be condemned."

38 Then some of the scribes and Pharisees answered him, saying, "Teacher, we wish to see a sign from you." 39 But he answered them, "An evil and adulterous generation seeks for a sign, but no sign will be given to it except the sign of the prophet Jonah. 40 For just as Jonah was three days and three nights in the belly of the great fish, so will the Son of Man be three days and three nights in the heart of the earth. 41 The men of Nineveh will rise up at the judgment with this generation and condemn it, for they repented at the preaching of Jonah, and behold, something greater than Jonah is here. 42 The queen of the South will rise up at the judgment with this generation and condemn it, for she came from the ends of the earth to hear the wisdom of Solomon, and behold, something greater than Solomon is here.

43 "When the unclean spirit has gone out of a person, it passes through waterless places seeking rest, but finds none. 44 Then it says, 'I will return to my house from which I came.' And when it comes, it finds the house empty, swept, and put in order. 45 Then it goes and brings with it seven other spirits more evil than itself, and they enter and dwell there, and the last state of that person

is worse than the first. So also will it be with this evil generation."

46 While he was still speaking to the people, behold, his mother and his brothers stood outside, asking to speak to him. 48 But he replied to the man who told him, "Who is my mother, and who are my brothers?" 49 And stretching out his hand toward his disciples, he said, "Here are my mother and my brothers! 50 For whoever does the will of my Father in heaven is my brother and sister and mother."

....

16:1 And the Pharisees and Sadducees came, and to test him they asked him to show them a sign from heaven. 2 He answered them, "When it is evening, you say, 'It will be fair weather, for the sky is red.' 3 And in the morning, 'It will be stormy today, for the sky is red and threatening.' You know how to interpret the appearance of the sky, but you cannot interpret the signs of the times. 4 An evil and adulterous generation seeks for a sign, but no sign will be given to it except the sign of Jonah." So he left them and departed.

1. In 12:38-42, what is it that prompts Jesus to talk about the "sign of the prophet Jonah"? What is the sign of Jonah?

2. What is the "something" that is greater than Jonah and wiser than Solomon? (Commentators say either the Kingdom of God or Jesus himself. What do you think?)

3. In verses 43-45, what does Jesus teach about "this evil generation" (see v. 45b)?

PONDER Prayerfully (and, if need be, repentantly) ponder verse 36.

PRAYER IDEAS Pray that the Holy Spirit may enable you to do the will of the Father this day.

READING 14   MATTHEW 13:1-23 ▢

That same day Jesus went out of the house and sat beside the sea. ² And great crowds gathered about him, so that he got into a boat and sat down. And the whole crowd stood on the beach. ³ And he told them many things in parables, saying: "A sower went out to sow. ⁴ And as he sowed, some seeds fell along the path, and the birds came and devoured them. ⁵ Other seeds fell on rocky ground, where they did not have much soil, and immediately they sprang up, since they had no depth of soil, ⁶ but when the sun rose they were scorched. And since they had no root, they withered away. ⁷ Other seeds fell among thorns, and the thorns grew up and choked them. ⁸ Other seeds fell on good soil and produced grain, some a hundredfold, some sixty, some thirty. ⁹ He who has ears, let him hear."

¹⁰ Then the disciples came and said to him, "Why do you speak to them in parables?" ¹¹ And he answered them, "To you it has been given to know the secrets of the kingdom of heaven, but to them it has not been given. ¹² For to the one who has, more will be given, and he will have an abundance, but from the one who has not, even what he has will be taken away. ¹³ This is why I speak to them in parables, because seeing they do not see, and hearing they do not hear, nor do they understand. ¹⁴ Indeed, in their case the prophecy of Isaiah is fulfilled that says:

"'You will indeed hear but never understand,
    and you will indeed see but never
        perceive.
¹⁵ For this people's heart has grown dull,
    and with their ears they can barely hear,
        and their eyes they have closed,
lest they should see with their eyes

and hear with their ears
and understand with their heart
and turn, and I would heal them.'

¹⁶ But blessed are your eyes, for they see, and your ears, for they hear. ¹⁷ Truly, I say to you, many prophets and righteous people longed to see what you see, and did not see it, and to hear what you hear, and did not hear it.

¹⁸ "Hear then the parable of the sower: ¹⁹ When anyone hears the word of the kingdom and does not understand it, the evil one comes and snatches away what has been sown in his heart. This is what was sown along the path. ²⁰ As for what was sown on rocky ground, this is the one who hears the word and immediately receives it with joy, ²¹ yet he has no root in himself, but endures for a while, and when tribulation or persecution arises on account of the word, immediately he falls away. ²² As for what was sown among thorns, this is the one who hears the word, but the cares of the world and the deceitfulness of riches choke the word, and it proves unfruitful. ²³ As for what was sown on good soil, this is the one who hears the word and understands it. He indeed bears fruit and yields, in one case a hundredfold, in another sixty, and in another thirty."

1. In verses 1-3, can you see any connection between the situation Jesus is in and the parable Jesus tells?

2. What reason does Jesus give for speaking in parables (vv. 11-15)?

3. *In verses 18-23, Jesus explains the four types of seed as four different responses to the preaching of the kingdom. Try finding a word to describe each of the four responses.*

PONDER Do you see any or all of those responses today? Which do you think is the most common response in our day?

PRAYER IDEAS Pray for people you know whose response to the gospel is like one of these four seeds. Pray that the Lord will give them ears to truly hear and minds to truly understand.

READING 15   MATTHEW 13:24-52

He put another parable before them, saying, "The kingdom of heaven may be compared to a man who sowed good seed in his field, 25 but while his men were sleeping, his enemy came and sowed weeds among the wheat and went away. 26 So when the plants came up and bore grain, then the weeds appeared also. 27 And the servants of the master of the house came and said to him, 'Master, did you not sow good seed in your field? How then does it have weeds?' 28 He said to them, 'An enemy has done this.' So the servants said to him, 'Then do you want us to go and gather them?' 29 But he said, 'No, lest in gathering the weeds you root up the wheat along with them. 30 Let both grow together until the harvest, and at harvest time I will tell the reapers, Gather the weeds first and bind them in bundles to be burned, but gather the wheat into my barn.'"

31 He put another parable before them, saying, "The kingdom of heaven is like a grain of mustard seed that a man took and sowed in his field. 32 It is the smallest of all seeds, but when it has grown it is larger than all the garden plants and becomes a tree, so that the birds of the air come and make nests in its branches."

33 He told them another parable. "The kingdom of heaven is like leaven that a woman took and hid in three measures of flour, till it was all leavened."

34 All these things Jesus said to the crowds in parables; indeed, he said nothing to them without a parable. 35 This was to fulfill what was spoken by the prophet:

"I will open my mouth in parables;
    I will utter what has been hidden since
        the foundation of the world."

36 Then he left the crowds and went into the house. And his disciples came to him, saying, "Explain to us the parable of the weeds of the field." 37 He answered, "The one who sows the good seed is the Son of Man. 38 The field is the world, and the good seed is the children of the kingdom. The weeds are the sons of the evil one, 39 and the enemy who sowed them is the devil. The harvest is the close of the age, and the reapers are angels. 40 Just as the weeds are gathered and burned with fire, so will it be at the close of the age. 41 The Son of Man will send his angels, and they will gather out of his kingdom all causes of sin and all law-breakers, 42 and throw them into the fiery furnace. In that place there will be weeping and gnashing of teeth. 43 Then the righteous will shine like the sun in the kingdom of their Father. He who has ears, let him hear.

44 "The kingdom of heaven is like treasure hidden in a field, which a man found and covered up. Then in his joy he goes and sells all that he has and buys that field.

45 "Again, the kingdom of heaven is like a merchant in search of fine pearls, 46 who, on

finding one pearl of great value, went and sold all that he had and bought it.

⁴⁷ "Again, the kingdom of heaven is like a net that was thrown into the sea and gathered fish of every kind. ⁴⁸ When it was full, men drew it ashore and sat down and sorted the good into containers but threw away the bad. ⁴⁹ So it will be at the close of the age. The angels will come out and separate the evil from the righteous ⁵⁰ and throw them into the fiery furnace. In that place there will be weeping and gnashing of teeth.

⁵¹ "Have you understood all these things?" They said to him, "Yes." ⁵² And he said to them, "Therefore every scribe who has been trained for the kingdom of heaven is like a master of a house, who brings out of his treasure what is new and what is old."

1. In verses 31-52, Jesus compares the kingdom of God to six different things.

Jot down all the things the kingdom is compared with.

2. Try writing your own statement of what Jesus is saying about the kingdom in each of those comparisons (note that verses 36-43 explain verses 24-30).

PONDER How do you react to these kingdom comparisons? Which do you find most unusual? Most attractive? Most unsettling?

PRAYER IDEAS Thank God that, in finding the kingdom, you have found a pearl of great price!

READING 16   MATTHEW 13:53-58

And when Jesus had finished these parables, he went away from there, ⁵⁴ and coming to his hometown he taught them in their synagogue, so that they were astonished, and said, "Where did this man get this wisdom and these mighty works? ⁵⁵ Is not this the carpenter's son? Is not his mother called Mary? And are not his brothers James and Joseph and Simon and Judas? ⁵⁶ And are not all his sisters with us? Where then did this man get all these things?" ⁵⁷ And they took offense at him. But Jesus said to them, "A prophet is not without honor except in his hometown and in his own household." ⁵⁸ And he did not do many mighty works there, because of their unbelief.

1. This section is a point where Matthew interrupts Jesus' teaching to tell us of a significant development in the story. What is that development?

2. What are the reactions to Jesus that Matthew records for us? How do those reactions fit with each other?

3. How does Jesus explain their reaction (v. 57)?

PONDER Do you see any of these responses to Jesus still in play today? Where?

PRAYER IDEAS Astonishment, incredulity, offence—these are all reactions we see to Jesus today. Pray that astonishment will turn to wonder, incredulity to faith, and offence to praise.

At that time Herod the tetrarch heard about the fame of Jesus, [2] and he said to his servants, "This is John the Baptist. He has been raised from the dead; that is why these miraculous powers are at work in him." [3] For Herod had seized John and bound him and put him in prison for the sake of Herodias, his brother Philip's wife, [4] because John had been saying to him, "It is not lawful for you to have her." [5] And though he wanted to put him to death, he feared the people, because they held him to be a prophet. [6] But when Herod's birthday came, the daughter of Herodias danced before the company and pleased Herod, [7] so that he promised with an oath to give her whatever she might ask. [8] Prompted by her mother, she said, "Give me the head of John the Baptist here on a platter." [9] And the king was sorry, but because of his oaths and his guests he commanded it to be given. [10] He sent and had John beheaded in the prison, [11] and his head was brought on a platter and given to the girl, and she brought it to her mother. [12] And his disciples came and took the body and buried it, and they went and told Jesus.

[13] Now when Jesus heard this, he withdrew from there in a boat to a desolate place by himself. But when the crowds heard it, they followed him on foot from the towns. [14] When he went ashore he saw a great crowd, and he had compassion on them and healed their sick. [15] Now when it was evening, the disciples came to him and said, "This is a desolate place, and the day is now over; send the crowds away to go into the villages and buy food for themselves." [16] But Jesus said, "They need not go away; you give them something to eat." [17] They said to him, "We have only five loaves here and two fish." [18] And he said, "Bring them here to me." [19] Then he ordered the crowds to sit down on the grass, and taking the five loaves and the two fish, he looked up to heaven and said a blessing.

Then he broke the loaves and gave them to the disciples, and the disciples gave them to the crowds. [20] And they all ate and were satisfied. And they took up twelve baskets full of the broken pieces left over. [21] And those who ate were about five thousand men, besides women and children.

[22] Immediately he made the disciples get into the boat and go before him to the other side, while he dismissed the crowds. [23] And after he had dismissed the crowds, he went up on the mountain by himself to pray. When evening came, he was there alone, [24] but the boat by this time was a long way from the land, beaten by the waves, for the wind was against them. [25] And in the fourth watch of the night he came to them, walking on the sea. [26] But when the disciples saw him walking on the sea, they were terrified, and said, "It is a ghost!" and they cried out in fear. [27] But immediately Jesus spoke to them, saying, "Take heart; it is I. Do not be afraid."

[28] And Peter answered him, "Lord, if it is you, command me to come to you on the water." [29] He said, "Come." So Peter got out of the boat and walked on the water and came to Jesus. [30] But when he saw the wind, he was afraid, and beginning to sink he cried out, "Lord, save me." [31] Jesus immediately reached out his hand and took hold of him, saying to him, "O you of little faith, why did you doubt?" [32] And when they got into the boat, the wind ceased. [33] And those in the boat worshiped him, saying, "Truly you are the Son of God."

[34] And when they had crossed over, they came to land at Gennesaret. [35] And when the men of that place recognized him, they sent around to all that region and brought to him all who were sick [36] and implored him that they might only touch the fringe of his garment. And as many as touched it were made well.

1. In recounting the story of John's death,

why do you think Matthew makes such a point of what happens to his body (see 14:2, 16:14,[5] 27:49[6])?

3. What do you think the climax of the 'walking on water' story is?

2. Verses 13-36 give details of Jesus' movements. Skim over the verses again, taking note of where Jesus goes (vv. 13, 14, 22, 23, 25, 34).

PONDER Consider the disarray of the world as we rule it, and consider the hope in seeing a man who rules it so well.

PRAYER IDEAS Pray for Jesus' return.

READING 18   MATTHEW 15:1-20

Then Pharisees and scribes came to Jesus from Jerusalem and said, 2 "Why do your disciples break the tradition of the elders? For they do not wash their hands when they eat." 3 He answered them, "And why do you break the commandment of God for the sake of your tradition? 4 For God commanded, 'Honor your father and your mother,' and, 'Whoever reviles father or mother must surely die.' 5 But you say, 'If anyone tells his father or his mother, What you would have gained from me is given to God, 6 he need not honor his father.' So for the sake of your tradition you have made void the word of God. 7 You hypocrites! Well did Isaiah prophesy of you, when he said:

8 "'This people honors me with their lips,
    but their heart is far from me;
9 in vain do they worship me,
    teaching as doctrines the
        commandments of men.'"

10 And he called the people to him and said to them, "Hear and understand: 11 it is not what goes into the mouth that defiles a person, but what comes out of the mouth; this defiles a person." 12 Then the disciples

came and said to him, "Do you know that the Pharisees were offended when they heard this saying?" 13 He answered, "Every plant that my heavenly Father has not planted will be rooted up. 14 Let them alone; they are blind guides. And if the blind lead the blind, both will fall into a pit." 15 But Peter said to him, "Explain the parable to us." 16 And he said, "Are you also still without understanding? 17 Do you not see that whatever goes into the mouth passes into the stomach and is expelled? 18 But what comes out of the mouth proceeds from the heart, and this defiles a person. 19 For out of the heart come evil thoughts, murder, adultery, sexual immorality, theft, false witness, slander. 20 These are what defile a person. But to eat with unwashed hands does not defile anyone."

1. What do the Pharisees and scribes accuse Jesus of breaking (v. 2)? What does Jesus accuse them of breaking? How would you describe the relationship between them?

---

5. And they said, "Some say John the Baptist, others say Elijah, and others Jeremiah or one of the prophets."

6. But the others said, "Wait, let us see whether Elijah will come to save him."

2. In verse 15, Peter asks Jesus to "explain the parable". Which parable is Peter talking about?

PONDER Jesus was, of course, speaking to a first-century Jewish context. Do you think you can observe similar things in a twenty-first-century Christian context?

3. In Jesus' explanation of the parable, what is the distinction he makes?

PRAYER IDEAS Sin is defiling—it makes a person unclean in heart. Thank God that, in the gospel, he has washed us clean.

READING 19   MATTHEW 15:21-39

And Jesus went away from there and withdrew to the district of Tyre and Sidon. 22 And behold, a Canaanite woman from that region came out and was crying, "Have mercy on me, O Lord, Son of David; my daughter is severely oppressed by a demon." 23 But he did not answer her a word. And his disciples came and begged him, saying, "Send her away, for she is crying out after us." 24 He answered, "I was sent only to the lost sheep of the house of Israel." 25 But she came and knelt before him, saying, "Lord, help me." 26 And he answered, "It is not right to take the children's bread and throw it to the dogs." 27 She said, "Yes, Lord, yet even the dogs eat the crumbs that fall from their masters' table." 28 Then Jesus answered her, "O woman, great is your faith! Be it done for you as you desire." And her daughter was healed instantly.

29 Jesus went on from there and walked beside the Sea of Galilee. And he went up on the mountain and sat down there. 30 And great crowds came to him, bringing with them the lame, the blind, the crippled, the mute, and many others, and they put them at his feet, and he healed them, 31 so that the crowd wondered, when they saw the mute speaking, the crippled healthy, the lame walking, and the blind seeing. And they glorified the God of Israel.

32 Then Jesus called his disciples to him and said, "I have compassion on the crowd because they have been with me now three days and have nothing to eat. And I am unwilling to send them away hungry, lest they faint on the way." 33 And the disciples said to him, "Where are we to get enough bread in such a desolate place to feed so great a crowd?" 34 And Jesus said to them, "How many loaves do you have?" They said, "Seven, and a few small fish." 35 And directing the crowd to sit down on the ground, 36 he took the seven loaves and the fish, and having given thanks he broke them and gave them to the disciples, and the disciples gave them to the crowds. 37 And they all ate and were satisfied. And they took up seven baskets full of the broken pieces left over. 38 Those who ate were four thousand men, besides women and children. 39 And after sending away the crowds, he got into the boat and went to the region of Magadan.

1. In verses 21-28 Jesus goes to the districts of Tyre and Sidon. Where have we heard of these places before? What do we know about them? (See Reading 9 on p. 16.)

2. In the passage, what is the significance of the woman being a Canaanite? In particular, what significance does Jesus draw from that fact (vv. 24, 26)?

3. Jesus has been astonished at someone's faith before (see 8:10[7]). What do the two instances have in common?

4. Verses 29-31 are almost a snapshot of what we have seen Jesus doing over the last month. Compare the language of these verses to that of 11:2-6.[8] What is Matthew drawing our attention to?

PONDER In these chapters, we see the pattern of Israel rejecting her Messiah, which will eventually lead to the gospel going to the Gentiles. Do you think of Israel's rejection of Jesus as having any implications for your self-understanding as a Christian?

PRAYER IDEAS "So do not become proud, but stand in awe" (Rom 11:20). Thank God that we Gentiles have been included in the mercy of God.

READING 20   MATTHEW 16:13-28

Now when Jesus came into the district of Caesarea Philippi, he asked his disciples, "Who do people say that the Son of Man is?" [14] And they said, "Some say John the Baptist, others say Elijah, and others Jeremiah or one of the prophets." [15] He said to them, "But who do you say that I am?" [16] Simon Peter replied, "You are the Christ, the Son of the living God." [17] And Jesus answered him, "Blessed are you, Simon Bar-Jonah! For flesh and blood has not revealed this to you, but my Father who is in heaven. [18] And I tell you, you are Peter, and on this rock will build my church, and the gates of hell shall not prevail against it. [19] I will give you the keys of the kingdom of heaven, and whatever you bind on earth shall be bound in heaven, and whatever you loose on earth shall be loosed in heaven." [20] Then he strictly charged the disciples to tell no one that he was the Christ.

[21] From that time Jesus began to show his disciples that he must go to Jerusalem and suffer many things from the elders and chief priests and scribes, and be killed, and on the third day be raised. [22] And Peter took him aside and began to rebuke him, saying, "Far be it from you, Lord! This shall never happen to you." [23] But he turned and said to Peter, "Get behind me, Satan! You are a hindrance to me. For you are not setting your mind on the things of God, but on the things of man."

[24] Then Jesus told his disciples, "If anyone would come after me, let him deny himself and take up his cross and follow me. [25] For whoever would save his life will lose it, but whoever loses his life for my sake will find it. [26] For what will it profit a man if he gains the whole world and forfeits his life? Or what shall a man give in return for his life? [27] For the Son of Man is going to come with his angels in the glory of his Father, and then he will repay each person according to what he has done. [28] Truly, I say to you, there are some standing here who will not taste death until they see the Son of Man coming in his kingdom."

---

7. When Jesus heard this, he marveled and said to those who followed him, "Truly, I tell you, with no one in Israel have I found such faith".
8. Now when John heard in prison about the deeds of the Christ, he sent word by his disciples [3] and said to him, "Are you the one who is to come, or shall we look for another?" [4] And Jesus answered them, "Go and tell John what you hear and see: [5] the blind receive their sight and the lame walk, lepers are cleansed and the deaf hear, and the dead are raised up, and the poor have good news preached to them. [6] And blessed is the one who is not offended by me."

1. What does Peter get right about Jesus (v. 16)? What does he get wrong (vv. 22-23)?

2. What does Jesus forecast for himself?

3. Given what Jesus' future holds, what does it mean to be his disciple?

PONDER Thinking back over chapters 8-16, take some time to jot down:

a) something new you have learnt

b) something challenging

c) something comforting

d) something that still perplexes you that you will keep trying to think through.

PRAYER IDEAS Thank God for his work in your life by his word in Matthew. Pray over new lessons you've learnt, old lessons you've been reminded of, words that have troubled you, and words that have comforted you.

NEHEMIAH

INTRODUCTION

From Genesis onwards, the historical books have traced the rise and fall of the nation of Israel. Nehemiah brings the story to an end. (The rest of the Old Testament contains 'Wisdom Literature'—books like Job, Psalms and Proverbs—and the words of the prophets, like Joel, Amos and Isaiah.) Nehemiah was a high official in the court of the Persian King. After Israel's return from exile (recorded in Ezra, the Bible book before Nehemiah), he helps with the process of rebuilding the nation, and especially the walls of the city of Jerusalem.

People say that Nehemiah is the book to read if you want to learn about leadership. But is it? People say Nehemiah is the book to read before you start out on a church building project. But is it?

Put aside all your preconceptions about this great Old Testament book, and read what really happens. Is Nehemiah's building project a success or a failure? Does his leadership have the desired effect? Maybe he's not the leader God's people really need at all!

This is a great book for reviewing the whole Old Testament story, and recognizing the way it highlights the need for the ultimate leader—the leader who can change hearts.

You might like to use this prayer before each of the next 20 studies:

Lord God,
You have brought us back from our slavery to sin, and written your law on our hearts by your Spirit. Teach us to obey you, to be faithful to you, as you are to us. As your church, enable us to maintain unity of the Spirit in the bond of peace, to your glory.
In the name of your Son,
Amen.

READING 21   THE STORY SO FAR ■

Genesis 12:1-7

Now the LORD said to Abram, "Go from your country and your kindred and your father's house to the land that I will show you. ² And I will make of you a great nation, and I will bless you and make your name great, so that you will be a blessing. ³ I will bless those who bless you, and him who dishonors you I will curse, and in you all the families of the earth shall be blessed."

⁴ So Abram went, as the LORD had told him, and Lot went with him. Abram was seventy-five years old when he departed from Haran. ⁵ And Abram took Sarai his wife, and Lot his brother's son, and all their possessions that they had gathered, and the people that they had acquired in Haran, and they set out to go to the land of Canaan. When they came to the land of Canaan, ⁶ Abram passed through the land to the place at Shechem, to

the oak of Moreh. At that time the Canaanites were in the land. ⁷ Then the LORD appeared to Abram and said, "To your offspring I will give this land." So he built there an altar to the LORD, who had appeared to him.

Deuteronomy 29:24–30:6

... all the nations will say, 'Why has the LORD done thus to this land? What caused the heat of this great anger?' ²⁵ Then people will say, 'It is because they abandoned the covenant of the LORD, the God of their fathers, which he made with them when he brought them out of the land of Egypt, ²⁶ and went and served other gods and worshiped them, gods whom they had not known and whom he had not allotted to them. ²⁷ Therefore the anger of the LORD was kindled against this land, bringing upon it all the curses written in this book, ²⁸ and the LORD uprooted them from their land in anger and fury and great wrath, and cast them into another land, as they are this day.'

²⁹ "The secret things belong to the LORD our God, but the things that are revealed belong to us and to our children forever, that we may do all the words of this law.

30:1 "And when all these things come upon you, the blessing and the curse, which I have set before you, and you call them to mind among all the nations where the LORD your God has driven you, ² and return to the LORD your God, you and your children, and obey his voice in all that I command you today, with all your heart and with all your soul, ³ then the LORD your God will restore your fortunes and have compassion on you, and he will gather you again from all the peoples where the LORD your God has scattered you. ⁴ If your outcasts are in the uttermost parts of heaven, from there the LORD your God will gather you, and from there he will take you. ⁵ And the LORD your God will bring you into the land that your fathers possessed, that you may possess it. And he will make you more prosperous and numerous than your fathers. ⁶ And the LORD your God will circumcise your heart and the heart of your offspring, so that you will love the LORD your God with all your heart and with all your soul, that you may live."

1. Read Genesis 12:1-7. What does God promise to do for Abram's descendants, and for the whole world?

2. Read Deuteronomy 29:24-30:6. As Israel is about to enter the Promised land, what warning does God give?

3. And what promise does God make?

PONDER How should these words of God make the recipients respond?

PRAYER IDEAS Pray that you (and others) would have this vision of God's Son constantly in your mind, that you would treat the Son as he deserves to be treated—as the Saving Lord of all.

READING 22   **NEHEMIAH 1**

The words of Nehemiah the son of Hacaliah. Now it happened in the month of Chislev, in the twentieth year, as I was in Susa the capital, ² that Hanani, one of my brothers, came with certain men from Judah. And I asked them concerning the Jews who escaped, who had survived the exile, and concerning Jerusalem. ³ And they said to me, "The remnant there in the province who had survived the exile is in great trouble and shame. The wall of Jerusalem is broken down, and its gates are destroyed by fire."

⁴ As soon as I heard these words I sat down and wept and mourned for days, and I continued fasting and praying before the God of heaven. ⁵ And I said, "O Lord God of heaven, the great and awesome God who keeps covenant and steadfast love with those who love him and keep his commandments, ⁶ let your ear be attentive and your eyes open, to hear the prayer of your servant that I now pray before you day and night for the people of Israel your servants, confessing the sins of the people of Israel, which we have sinned against you. Even I and my father's house have sinned. ⁷ We have acted very corruptly against you and have not kept the commandments, the statutes, and the rules that you commanded your servant Moses. ⁸ Remember the word that you commanded your servant Moses, saying, 'If you are unfaithful, I will scatter you among the peoples, ⁹ but if you return to me and keep my commandments and do them, though your dispersed be under the farthest skies, I will gather them from there and bring them to the place that I have chosen, to make my name dwell there.' ¹⁰ They are your servants and your people, whom you have redeemed by your great power and by your strong hand. ¹¹ O Lord, let your ear be attentive to the prayer of your servant, and to the prayer of your servants who delight to fear your name, and give success to your servant today, and grant him mercy in the sight of this man."

Now I was cupbearer to the king.

1. What situation is Nehemiah in as he writes?

2. The book of Nehemiah is written a little like a diary. In chapter 1, what do we learn about Nehemiah, the man?

3. Summarize Nehemiah's request to God.

4. What is the required starting point for Israel's new relationship with God (v. 9)?

PONDER Nehemiah weeps because of his sin, but all the while remembers God's promises of restoration. Is this how you approach God?

PRAYER IDEAS Confess to God the times you have abandoned his ways. Thank him for his promises to those who believe.

READING 23   NEHEMIAH 2 ▢

In the month of Nisan, in the twentieth year of King Artaxerxes, when wine was before him, I took up the wine and gave it to the king. Now I had not been sad in his presence. ² And the king said to me, "Why is your face sad, seeing you are not sick? This is nothing but sadness of the heart." Then I was very much afraid. ³ I said to the king, "Let the king live forever! Why should not my face be sad, when the city, the place of my fathers' graves, lies in ruins, and its gates have been destroyed by fire?" ⁴ Then the king said to me, "What are you requesting?" So I prayed to the God of heaven. ⁵ And I said to the king, "If it pleases the king, and if your servant has found favor in your sight, that you send me to Judah, to the city of my fathers' graves, that I may rebuild it." ⁶ And the king said to me (the queen sitting beside him), "How long will you be gone, and when will you return?" So it pleased the king to send me when I had given him a time. ⁷ And

I said to the king, "If it pleases the king, let letters be given me to the governors of the province Beyond the River, that they may let me pass through until I come to Judah, [8] and a letter to Asaph, the keeper of the king's forest, that he may give me timber to make beams for the gates of the fortress of the temple, and for the wall of the city, and for the house that I shall occupy." And the king granted me what I asked, for the good hand of my God was upon me.

[9] Then I came to the governors of the province Beyond the River and gave them the king's letters. Now the king had sent with me officers of the army and horsemen. [10] But when Sanballat the Horonite and Tobiah, the Ammonite servant, heard this, it displeased them greatly that someone had come to seek the welfare of the people of Israel.

[11] So I went to Jerusalem and was there three days. [12] Then I arose in the night, I and a few men with me. And I told no one what my God had put into my heart to do for Jerusalem. There was no animal with me but the one on which I rode. [13] I went out by night by the Valley Gate to the Dragon Spring and to the Dung Gate, and I inspected the walls of Jerusalem that were broken down and its gates that had been destroyed by fire. [14] Then I went on to the Fountain Gate and to the King's Pool, but there was no room for the animal that was under me to pass. [15] Then I went up in the night by the valley and inspected the wall, and I turned back and entered by the Valley Gate, and so returned. [16] And the officials did not know where I had gone or what I was doing, and I had not yet told the Jews, the priests, the nobles, the officials, and the rest who were to do the work.

[17] Then I said to them, "You see the trouble we are in, how Jerusalem lies in ruins with its gates burned. Come, let us build the wall of Jerusalem, that we may no longer suffer derision." [18] And I told them of the hand of my God that had been upon me for good, and also of the words that the king had spoken to me. And they said, "Let us rise up and build." So they strengthened their hands for the good work. [19] But when Sanballat the Horonite and Tobiah the Ammonite servant and Geshem the Arab heard of it, they jeered at us and despised us and said, "What is this thing that you are doing? Are you rebelling against the king?" [20] Then I replied to them, "The God of heaven will make us prosper, and we his servants will arise and build, but you have no portion or right or claim in Jerusalem."

1. What does Nehemiah want to do, and why?

2. What are Sanballat and Tobiah worried about (v. 10)? Keep your eye on these guys right through the book!

3. What is Nehemiah's confidence of success based on (vv. 18, 20)?

PONDER Why do the Israelites want to rebuild the walls of Jerusalem?

PRAYER IDEAS Thank God for his goodness and faithfulness to his people.

READING 24   NEHEMIAH 3 ▢

Then Eliashib the high priest rose up with his brothers the priests, and they built the Sheep Gate. They consecrated it and set its doors. They consecrated it as far as the Tower of the Hundred, as far as the Tower of Hananel. [2] And next to him the men of Jericho built. And next to them Zaccur the son of Imri built. [3] The sons of Hassenaah built the Fish Gate.

They laid its beams and set its doors, its bolts, and its bars. [4] And next to them Meremoth the son of Uriah, son of Hakkoz repaired. And next to them Meshullam the son of Berechiah, son of Meshezabel repaired. And next to them Zadok the son of Baana repaired. [5] And next to them the Tekoites repaired, but their nobles would not stoop to serve their Lord.

[6] Joiada the son of Paseah and Meshullam the son of Besodeiah repaired the Gate of Yeshanah. They laid its beams and set its doors, its bolts, and its bars. [7] And next to them repaired Melatiah the Gibeonite and Jadon the Meronothite, the men of Gibeon and of Mizpah, the seat of the governor of the province Beyond the River. [8] Next to them Uzziel the son of Harhaiah, goldsmiths, repaired. Next to him Hananiah, one of the perfumers, repaired, and they restored Jerusalem as far as the Broad Wall. [9] Next to them Rephaiah the son of Hur, ruler of half the district of Jerusalem, repaired. [10] Next to them Jedaiah the son of Harumaph repaired opposite his house. And next to him Hattush the son of Hashabneiah repaired. [11] Malchijah the son of Harim and Hasshub the son of Pahath-moab repaired another section and the Tower of the Ovens. [12] Next to him Shallum the son of Hallohesh, ruler of half the district of Jerusalem, repaired, he and his daughters.

[13] Hanun and the inhabitants of Zanoah repaired the Valley Gate. They rebuilt it and set its doors, its bolts, and its bars, and repaired a thousand cubits of the wall, as far as the Dung Gate.

[14] Malchijah the son of Rechab, ruler of the district of Beth-haccherem, repaired the Dung Gate. He rebuilt it and set its doors, its bolts, and its bars.

[15] And Shallum the son of Col-hozeh, ruler of the district of Mizpah, repaired the Fountain Gate. He rebuilt it and covered it and set its doors, its bolts, and its bars. And he built the wall of the Pool of Shelah of the king's garden, as far as the stairs that go down from the City of David. [16] After him Nehemiah the son of Azbuk, ruler of half the district of Beth-zur, repaired to a point opposite the tombs of David, as far as the artificial pool, and as far as the house of the mighty men. [17] After him the Levites repaired: Rehum the son of Bani. Next to him Hashabiah, ruler of half the district of Keilah, repaired for his district. [18] After him their brothers repaired: Bavvai the son of Henadad, ruler of half the district of Keilah. [19] Next to him Ezer the son of Jeshua, ruler of Mizpah, repaired another section opposite the ascent to the armory at the buttress. [20] After him Baruch the son of Zabbai repaired another section from the buttress to the door of the house of Eliashib the high priest. [21] After him Meremoth the son of Uriah, son of Hakkoz repaired another section from the door of the house of Eliashib to the end of the house of Eliashib. [22] After him the priests, the men of the surrounding area, repaired. [23] After them Benjamin and Hasshub repaired opposite their house. After them Azariah the son of Maaseiah, son of Ananiah repaired beside his own house. [24] After him Binnui the son of Henadad repaired another section, from the house of Azariah to the buttress [25] and to the corner. Palal the son of Uzai repaired opposite the buttress and the tower projecting from the upper house of the king at the court of the guard. After him Pedaiah the son of Parosh [26] and the temple servants living on Ophel repaired to a point opposite the Water Gate on the east and the projecting tower. [27] After him the Tekoites repaired another section opposite the great projecting tower as far as the wall of Ophel.

[28] Above the Horse Gate the priests repaired, each one opposite his own house. [29] After them Zadok the son of Immer repaired opposite his own house. After him Shemaiah the son of Shecaniah, the keeper of the East Gate, repaired. [30] After him Hananiah the son of Shelemiah and Hanun the sixth son of Zalaph repaired another section. After him

Meshullam the son of Berechiah repaired opposite his chamber. ³¹ After him Malchijah, one of the goldsmiths, repaired as far as the house of the temple servants and of the merchants, opposite the Muster Gate, and to the upper chamber of the corner. ³² And between the upper chamber of the corner and the Sheep Gate the goldsmiths and the merchants repaired.

1. *Nehemiah 3 is a long and detailed account of the rebuilding of Jerusalem's walls. As you read, imagine you're on a tour of a building site. You begin at the sheep gate, move past the towers, the Fish gate, and the Valley Gate. (Spare a thought for the builders at the Dung Gate.) You'll read the details of the doors, the bolts, and the beams. Notice the tour ends at the Sheep Gate, where it began.*

2. *Which people did this repair work?*

3. *Was there anyone who refused to help?*

PONDER Most church working bees struggle to get more than half a dozen people involved. What does the list of names tell you about the attitude of the Israelites?

PRAYER IDEAS Ask that God might strengthen your commitment to doing his work in the world.

POINTER This chapter summarizes the building of the wall around Jerusalem, which is described in more detail from chapters 4–6:15.

READING 25 NEHEMIAH 4:1-5

Now when Sanballat heard that we were building the wall, he was angry and greatly enraged, and he jeered at the Jews. ² And he said in the presence of his brothers and of the army of Samaria, "What are these feeble Jews doing? Will they restore it for themselves? Will they sacrifice? Will they finish up in a day? Will they revive the stones out of the heaps of rubbish, and burned ones at that?" ³ Tobiah the Ammonite was beside him, and he said, "Yes, what they are building—if a fox goes up on it he will break down their stone wall!" ⁴ Hear, O our God, for we are despised. Turn back their taunt on their own heads and give them up to be plundered in a land where they are captives. ⁵ Do not cover their guilt, and let not their sin be blotted out from your sight, for they have provoked you to anger in the presence of the builders.

1. *What are Sanballat and Tobiah's objections?*

2. *Is Nehemiah's prayer in verse 4 reasonable? How does he perceive the situation?*

3. *In what ways have Sanballat and Tobiah angered God?*

PONDER When God's people are mocked, God himself is mocked. This is a strong theme throughout the Bible, culminating in the humiliation of the cross.

PRAYER IDEAS Pray that God will honour his name and bring his enemies to account.

So we built the wall. And all the wall was joined together to half its height, for the people had a mind to work.

[7] But when Sanballat and Tobiah and the Arabs and the Ammonites and the Ashdodites heard that the repairing of the walls of Jerusalem was going forward and that the breaches were beginning to be closed, they were very angry. [8] And they all plotted together to come and fight against Jerusalem and to cause confusion in it. [9] And we prayed to our God and set a guard as a protection against them day and night.

[10] In Judah it was said, "The strength of those who bear the burdens is failing. There is too much rubble. By ourselves we will not be able to rebuild the wall." [11] And our enemies said, "They will not know or see till we come among them and kill them and stop the work." [12] At that time the Jews who lived near them came from all directions and said to us ten times, "You must return to us." [13] So in the lowest parts of the space behind the wall, in open places, I stationed the people by their clans, with their swords, their spears, and their bows. [14] And I looked and arose and said to the nobles and to the officials and to the rest of the people, "Do not be afraid of them. Remember the Lord, who is great and awesome, and fight for your brothers, your sons, your daughters, your wives, and your homes."

1. What two threats emerge to hamper the completion of the wall?
-
-

2. How do the Israelites gather their strength (vv. 9, 14)?

PONDER In times of hardship, do you find strength in previous occasions when you have 'remembered the Lord' and endured or persevered?

PRAYER IDEAS Pray that you will always recall the greatness and awesomeness of God when you face opposition.

When our enemies heard that it was known to us and that God had frustrated their plan, we all returned to the wall, each to his work. [16] From that day on, half of my servants worked on construction, and half held the spears, shields, bows, and coats of mail. And the leaders stood behind the whole house of Judah, [17] who were building on the wall. Those who carried burdens were loaded in such a way that each labored on the work with one hand and held his weapon with the other. [18] And each of the builders had his sword strapped at his side while he built. The man who sounded the trumpet was beside me. [19] And I said to the nobles and to the officials and to the rest of the people, "The work is great and widely spread, and we are separated on the wall, far from one another. [20] In the place where you hear the sound of the trumpet, rally to us there. Our God will fight for us."

[21] So we labored at the work, and half of them held the spears from the break of dawn until the stars came out. [22] I also said to the people at that time, "Let every man and his servant pass the night within Jerusalem, that they may be a guard for us by night and may labor by day." [23] So neither I nor my brothers nor my servants nor the men of the guard who followed me, none of us took off our clothes; each kept his weapon at his right hand.

1. How would you describe the manner in which the Israelites work?

2. What confident claim does Nehemiah make in verse 20?

3. Some churches study the book of Nehemiah before they launch a building program, and assume that because God was behind Nehemiah's rebuilding project, he'll back up our modern day schemes—if only we have enough faith. What is wrong with this approach to God's promises?

PONDER Read 2 Corinthians 1:20.[9] How does this verse help us to understand the current status of the promises God gave in the Old Testament?

PRAYER IDEAS Thank God for the fulfilment of all of his promises in the death, resurrection and ascension of Jesus.

POINTER The relationship between the Old Testament promises and the gospel is multi-faceted. Two other passages worth pondering are Galatians 3:16-22 and Romans 4:1-12 (printed in the appendix on pp. 74-75). We will return to these ideas later in these studies.

READING 28   NEHEMIAH 5:1-13

Now there arose a great outcry of the people and of their wives against their Jewish brothers. 2 For there were those who said, "With our sons and our daughters, we are many. So let us get grain, that we may eat and keep alive." 3 There were also those who said, "We are mortgaging our fields, our vineyards, and our houses to get grain because of the famine." 4 And there were those who said, "We have borrowed money for the king's tax on our fields and our vineyards. 5 Now our flesh is as the flesh of our brothers, our children are as their children. Yet we are forcing our sons and our daughters to be slaves, and some of our daughters have already been enslaved, but it is not in our power to help it, for other men have our fields and our vineyards."

6 I was very angry when I heard their outcry and these words. 7 I took counsel with myself, and I brought charges against the nobles and the officials. I said to them, "You are exacting interest, each from his brother."

And I held a great assembly against them 8 and said to them, "We, as far as we are able, have bought back our Jewish brothers who have been sold to the nations, but you even sell your brothers that they may be sold to us!" They were silent and could not find a word to say. 9 So I said, "The thing that you are doing is not good. Ought you not to walk in the fear of our God to prevent the taunts of the nations our enemies? 10 Moreover, I and my brothers and my servants are lending them money and grain. Let us abandon this exacting of interest. 11 Return to them this very day their fields, their vineyards, their olive orchards, and their houses, and the percentage of money, grain, wine, and oil that you have been exacting from them." 12 Then they said, "We will restore these and require nothing from them. We will do as you say." And I called the priests and made them swear to do as they had promised. 13 I also shook out the fold of my garment and said, "So may God shake out every man from his house and from his

---

9. For all the promises of God find their Yes in him. That is why it is through him that we utter our Amen to God for his glory.

labor who does not keep this promise. So may he be shaken out and emptied." And all the assembly said "Amen" and praised the LORD. And the people did as they had promised.

1. *Israel's attacks have always come from the inside as much as from the outside. How have they been abusing each other?*

2. *What is Nehemiah's proposed solution (vv. 9-11)?*

3. *How does the situation get resolved (vv. 12-13)?*

PONDER 'Usury' is extracting unfair interest on a loan, taking advantage of a weaker party. The Israelite nobles are taking advantage of their countrymen in a way that even their enemies would have been ashamed of! Do Christians today sin in this way?

PRAYER IDEAS Pray that God will enable you to treat your fellow believers with love and generosity, not using them for your own gain.

READING 29   NEHEMIAH 5:14-19 ☐

Moreover, from the time that I was appointed to be their governor in the land of Judah, from the twentieth year to the thirty-second year of Artaxerxes the king, twelve years, neither I nor my brothers ate the food allowance of the governor. [15] The former governors who were before me laid heavy burdens on the people and took from them for their daily ration forty shekels of silver. Even their servants lorded it over the people. But I did not do so, because of the fear of God. [16] I also persevered in the work on this wall, and we acquired no land, and all my servants were gathered there for the work. [17] Moreover, there were at my table 150 men, Jews and officials, besides those who came to us from the nations that were around us. [18] Now what was prepared at my expense for each day was one ox and six choice sheep and birds, and every ten days all kinds of wine in abundance. Yet for all this I did not demand the food allowance of the governor, because the service was too heavy on this people. [19] Remember for my good, O my God, all that I have done for this people.

1. *Why wouldn't Nehemiah accept the food allowance of the governor?*

2. *For what purpose does Nehemiah want God to remember his deeds (v. 19)?*

3. *Read 1 Peter 5:1-6.[10] How has Christ illustrated the fact that leadership is sacrificial? How should Christian leaders today reflect this?*

---

10. So I exhort the elders among you, as a fellow elder and a witness of the sufferings of Christ, as well as a partaker in the glory that is going to be revealed: [2] shepherd the flock of God that is among you, exercising oversight, not under compulsion, but willingly, as God would have you; not for shameful gain, but eagerly; [3] not domineering over those in your charge, but being examples to the flock. [4] And when the chief Shepherd appears, you will receive the unfading crown of glory. [5] Likewise, you who are younger, be subject to the elders. Clothe yourselves, all of you, with humility toward one another, for "God opposes the proud but gives grace to the humble."
[6] Humble yourselves, therefore, under the mighty hand of God so that at the proper time he may exalt you ...

PONDER In your own church and ministries, are there any ways in which the leaders are placing too heavy a burden on those whom they lead? What can be done about this?

PRAYER IDEAS Pray that your leaders will be humble, generous, and self-sacrificing. Pray that they will also be well provided for by those they serve.

READING 30   ·   NEHEMIAH 6:1-14

Now when Sanballat and Tobiah and Geshem the Arab and the rest of our enemies heard that I had built the wall and that there was no breach left in it (although up to that time I had not set up the doors in the gates), ² Sanballat and Geshem sent to me, saying, "Come and let us meet together at Hakkephirim in the plain of Ono." But they intended to do me harm. ³ And I sent messengers to them, saying, "I am doing a great work and I cannot come down. Why should the work stop while I leave it and come down to you?" ⁴ And they sent to me four times in this way, and I answered them in the same manner. ⁵ In the same way Sanballat for the fifth time sent his servant to me with an open letter in his hand. ⁶ In it was written, "It is reported among the nations, and Geshem also says it, that you and the Jews intend to rebel; that is why you are building the wall. And according to these reports you wish to become their king. ⁷ And you have also set up prophets to proclaim concerning you in Jerusalem, 'There is a king in Judah.' And now the king will hear of these reports. So now come and let us take counsel together." ⁸ Then I sent to him, saying, "No such things as you say have been done, for you are inventing them out of your own mind." ⁹ For they all wanted to frighten us, thinking, "Their hands will drop from the work, and it will not be done." But now, O God, strengthen my hands.

¹⁰ Now when I went into the house of Shemaiah the son of Delaiah, son of Mehetabel, who was confined to his home, he said, "Let us meet together in the house of God, within the temple. Let us close the doors of the temple, for they are coming to kill you. They are coming to kill you by night." ¹¹ But I said, "Should such a man as I run away? And what man such as I could go into the temple and live? I will not go in." ¹² And I understood and saw that God had not sent him, but he had pronounced the prophecy against me because Tobiah and Sanballat had hired him. ¹³ For this purpose he was hired, that I should be afraid and act in this way and sin, and so they could give me a bad name in order to taunt me. ¹⁴ Remember Tobiah and Sanballat, O my God, according to these things that they did, and also the prophetess Noadiah and the rest of the prophets who wanted to make me afraid.

1. What strategy do Sanballat and Tobiah use now to try to trap Nehemiah?

2. In what way was Shemaiah's offer a trap? (See Num 3:10¹¹ and 38.¹²) N.B. Nehemiah is not a Levite.

3. How does Nehemiah know the prophecy isn't genuine?

---

11. "And you shall appoint Aaron and his sons, and they shall guard their priesthood. But if any outsider comes near, he shall be put to death."
12. Those who were to camp before the tabernacle on the east, before the tent of meeting toward the sunrise, were Moses and Aaron and his sons, guarding the sanctuary itself, to protect the people of Israel. And any outsider who came near was to be put to death.

PRAYER IDEAS The tests of true prophecy are very clear in the New Testament. Read 1 John 4:1-3.[13] How would you test a prophetic claim?

PRAYER IDEAS Ask God to strengthen your trust in his word, by which we can know the truth.

READING 31   NEHEMIAH 6:15-7:4

So the wall was finished on the twenty-fifth day of the month Elul, in fifty-two days. [16] And when all our enemies heard of it, all the nations around us were afraid and fell greatly in their own esteem, for they perceived that this work had been accomplished with the help of our God. [17] Moreover, in those days the nobles of Judah sent many letters to Tobiah, and Tobiah's letters came to them. [18] For many in Judah were bound by oath to him, because he was the son-in-law of Shecaniah the son of Arah: and his son Jehohanan had taken the daughter of Meshullam the son of Berechiah as his wife. [19] Also they spoke of his good deeds in my presence and reported my words to him. And Tobiah sent letters to make me afraid.

7:1 Now when the wall had been built and I had set up the doors, and the gatekeepers, the singers, and the Levites had been appointed, [2] I gave my brother Hanani and Hananiah the governor of the castle charge over Jerusalem, for he was a more faithful and God-fearing man than many. [3] And I said to them, "Let not the gates of Jerusalem be opened until the sun is hot. And while they are still standing guard, let them shut and bar the doors. Appoint guards from among the inhabitants of Jerusalem, some at their guard posts and some in front of their own homes." [4] The city was wide and large, but the people within it were few, and no houses had been rebuilt.

1. The completion of the Jerusalem city wall took 52 days of hard work. Who is afraid now? Why?

2. Internal troubles arise again from the Jewish nobles. What potential problem exists?

3. What kind of men does Nehemiah appoint to protect the completed wall?

PONDER A leader needs to not only pursue what is right, but also prevent what is wrong.

PRAYER IDEAS Pray that God will protect your church groups from disunity and 'serving two masters'.

POINTER Tobiah was related to a number of the Jews, via Shecaniah and Meshullam's daughter (v. 18). Meshullam was one of the leading wall-builders (see 3:4,[14] 30[15]).

---

13. Beloved, do not believe every spirit, but test the spirits to see whether they are from God, for many false prophets have gone out into the world. [2] By this you know the Spirit of God: every spirit that confesses that Jesus Christ has come in the flesh is from God, [3] and every spirit that does not confess Jesus is not from God. This is the spirit of the antichrist, which you heard was coming and now is in the world already.

14. And next to them Meremoth the son of Uriah, son of Hakkoz repaired. And next to them Meshullam the son of Berechiah, son of Meshezabel repaired. And next to them Zadok the son of Baana repaired.
15. After him Hananiah the son of Shelemiah and Hanun the sixth son of Zalaph repaired another section. After him Meshullam the son of Berechiah repaired opposite his chamber.

Now when the wall had been built and I had set up the doors, and the gatekeepers, the singers, and the Levites had been appointed, [2] I gave my brother Hanani and Hananiah the governor of the castle charge over Jerusalem, for he was a more faithful and God-fearing man than many. [3] And I said to them, "Let not the gates of Jerusalem be opened until the sun is hot. And while they are still standing guard, let them shut and bar the doors. Appoint guards from among the inhabitants of Jerusalem, some at their guard posts and some in front of their own homes." [4] The city was wide and large, but the people within it were few, and no houses had been rebuilt.

[5] Then my God put it into my heart to assemble the nobles and the officials and the people to be enrolled by genealogy. And I found the book of the genealogy of those who came up at the first, and I found written in it:

[6] These were the people of the province who came up out of the captivity of those exiles whom Nebuchadnezzar the king of Babylon had carried into exile. They returned to Jerusalem and Judah, each to his town. [7] They came with Zerubbabel, Jeshua, Nehemiah, Azariah, Raamiah, Nahamani, Mordecai, Bilshan, Mispereth, Bigvai, Nehum, Baanah.

The number of the men of the people of Israel: [8] the sons of Parosh, 2,172. [9] The sons of Shephatiah, 372. [10] The sons of Arah, 652. [11] The sons of Pahath-moab, namely the sons of Jeshua and Joab, 2,818. [12] The sons of Elam, 1,254. [13] The sons of Zattu, 845. [14] The sons of Zaccai, 760. [15] The sons of Binnui, 648. [16] The sons of Bebai, 628. [17] The sons of Azgad, 2,322. [18] The sons of Adonikam, 667. [19] The sons of Bigvai, 2,067. [20] The sons of Adin, 655. [21] The sons of Ater, namely of Hezekiah, 98. [22] The sons of Hashum, 328. [23] The sons of Bezai, 324. [24] The sons of Hariph, 112. [25] The sons of Gibeon, 95. [26] The men of Bethlehem and Netophah, 188. [27] The men of Anathoth, 128. [28] The men of Beth-azmaveth, 42. [29] The men of Kiriath-jearim, Chephirah, and Beeroth, 743. [30] The men of Ramah and Geba, 621. [31] The men of Michmas, 122. [32] The men of Bethel and Ai, 123. [33] The men of the other Nebo, 52. [34] The sons of the other Elam, 1,254. [35] The sons of Harim, 320. [36] The sons of Jericho, 345. [37] The sons of Lod, Hadid, and Ono, 721. [38] The sons of Senaah, 3,930.

[39] The priests: the sons of Jedaiah, namely the house of Jeshua, 973. [40] The sons of Immer, 1,052. [41] The sons of Pashhur, 1,247. [42] The sons of Harim, 1,017.

[43] The Levites: the sons of Jeshua, namely of Kadmiel of the sons of Hodevah, 74.

[44] The singers: the sons of Asaph, 148. [45] The gatekeepers: the sons of Shallum, the sons of Ater, the sons of Talmon, the sons of Akkub, the sons of Hatita, the sons of Shobai, 138.

[46] The temple servants: the sons of Ziha, the sons of Hasupha, the sons of Tabbaoth, [47] the sons of Keros, the sons of Sia, the sons of Padon, [48] the sons of Lebana, the sons of Hagaba, the sons of Shalmai, [49] the sons of Hanan, the sons of Giddel, the sons of Gahar, [50] the sons of Reaiah, the sons of Rezin, the sons of Nekoda, [51] the sons of Gazzam, the sons of Uzza, the sons of Paseah, [52] the sons of Besai, the sons of Meunim, the sons of Nephushesim, [53] the sons of Bakbuk, the sons of Hakupha, the sons of Harhur, [54] the sons of Bazlith, the sons of Mehida, the sons of Harsha, [55] the sons of Barkos, the sons of Sisera, the sons of Temah, [56] the sons of Neziah, the sons of Hatipha.

[57] The sons of Solomon's servants: the sons of Sotai, the sons of Sophereth, the sons of Perida, [58] the sons of Jaala, the sons of Darkon, the sons of Giddel, [59] the sons of Shephatiah, the sons of Hattil, the sons of Pochereth-hazzebaim, the sons of Amon.

[60] All the temple servants and the sons of Solomon's servants were 392.

[61] The following were those who came up

from Tel-melah, Tel-harsha, Cherub, Addon, and Immer, but they could not prove their fathers' houses nor their descent, whether they belonged to Israel: 62 the sons of Delaiah, the sons of Tobiah, the sons of Nekoda, 642. 63 Also, of the priests: the sons of Hobaiah, the sons of Hakkoz, the sons of Barzillai (who had taken a wife of the daughters of Barzillai the Gileadite and was called by their name). 64 These sought their registration among those enrolled in the genealogies, but it was not found there, so they were excluded from the priesthood as unclean. 65 The governor told them that they were not to partake of the most holy food until a priest with Urim and Thummim should arise.

66 The whole assembly together was 42,360, 67 besides their male and female servants, of whom there were 7,337. And they had 245 singers, male and female. 68 Their horses were 736, their mules 245, 69 their camels 435, and their donkeys 6,720.

70 Now some of the heads of fathers' houses gave to the work. The governor gave to the treasury 1,000 darics of gold, 50 basins, 30 priests' garments and 500 minas of silver. 71 And some of the heads of fathers' houses gave into the treasury of the work 20,000 darics of gold and 2,200 minas of silver. 72 And what the rest of the people gave was 20,000 darics of gold, 2,000 minas of silver, and 67 priests' garments.

73 So the priests, the Levites, the gatekeepers, the singers, some of the people, the temple servants, and all Israel, lived in their towns.

And when the seventh month had come, the people of Israel were in their towns.

1. Did Nehemiah decide himself who would return to Israel (vv. 5-6)?

2. Quickly read the list of the sons of Israel in chapter 7. Verses 61 and 64 highlight an important point. Why is it so important that these people prove their lineage?

3. What overall impact does it have to read the many details of the returning exiles?

PONDER God's promise to restore his penitent people has been fulfilled. But is their repentance genuine? How would you recognize genuine repentance?

PRAYER IDEAS Thank God that he kept his promise to restore the people of Israel to its own land at that time.

READING 33   NEHEMIAH 8:1-12

And all the people gathered as one man into the square before the Water Gate. And they told Ezra the scribe to bring the Book of the Law of Moses that the LORD had commanded Israel. 2 So Ezra the priest brought the Law before the assembly, both men and women and all who could understand what they heard, on the first day of the seventh month. 3 And he read from it facing the square before the Water Gate from early morning until midday, in the presence of the men and the women and those who could understand. And the ears of all the people were attentive to the Book of the Law. 4 And Ezra the scribe stood on a wooden platform that they had made for the purpose. And beside him stood Mattithiah, Shema, Anaiah, Uriah, Hilkiah, and Maaseiah on his right hand, and Pedaiah, Mishael, Malchijah, Hashum, Hashbaddanah, Zechariah, and Meshullam on his left hand. 5 And Ezra opened the book in the sight of all the people, for he was above all the people, and as he opened it all the people stood. [6] And Ezra blessed the LORD, the great God, and all the people answered, "Amen, Amen," lifting up their hands. And they bowed their heads and worshiped the LORD with their faces to the ground. [7] Also Jeshua, Bani, Sherebiah, Jamin, Akkub, Shabbethai, Hodiah, Maaseiah, Kelita, Azariah, Jozabad, Hanan, Pelaiah, the Levites, helped the people to understand the Law, while the people remained in their places. [8] They read from the book, from the Law of God, clearly, and they gave the sense, so that the people understood the reading.

[9] And Nehemiah, who was the governor, and Ezra the priest and scribe, and the Levites who taught the people said to all the people, "This day is holy to the LORD your God; do not mourn or weep." For all the people wept as they heard the words of the Law. [10] Then he said to them, "Go your way. Eat the fat and drink sweet wine and send portions to anyone who has nothing ready, for this day is holy to our Lord. And do not be grieved, for the joy of the LORD is your strength." [11] So the Levites calmed all the people, saying, "Be quiet, for this day is holy; do not be grieved." [12] And all the people went their way to eat and drink and to send portions and to make great rejoicing, because they had understood the words that were declared to them.

1. There is a great sense of occasion here, as Ezra reads from the Book of the Law of Moses. How do the people respond in verse 6?

2. What do the Levites do?

3. The Israelites weep when they hear God's word. Why? Could it be connected with the events of 6:17-19?[16]

PONDER If Israel has fallen short of God's standards, why does Nehemiah insist that this is a day for rejoicing rather than mourning?

PRAYER IDEAS Praise God for his Word, which reveals to us our sinfulness and his steadfast love.

READING 34   NEHEMIAH 8:13-18

On the second day the heads of fathers' houses of all the people, with the priests and the Levites, came together to Ezra the scribe in order to study the words of the Law. [14] And they found it written in the Law that the LORD had commanded by Moses that the people of Israel should dwell in booths during the feast of the seventh month, [15] and that they should proclaim it and publish it in all their towns and in Jerusalem, "Go out to the hills and bring branches of olive, wild olive, myrtle, palm, and other leafy trees to make booths, as it is written." [16] So the people went out and brought them and made booths for themselves, each on his roof, and in their courts and in the courts of the house of God, and in the square at the Water Gate and in the square at the Gate of Ephraim. [17] And all the assembly of those who had returned from the captivity made booths and lived in the booths, for from the days of Jeshua the son of Nun to that day

---

16. Moreover, in those days the nobles of Judah sent many letters to Tobiah, and Tobiah's letters came to them. [18] For many in Judah were bound by oath to him, because he was the son-in-law of Shecaniah the son of Arah: and his son Jehohanan had taken the daughter of Meshullam the son of Berechiah as his wife. [19] Also they spoke of his good deeds in my presence and reported my words to him. And Tobiah sent letters to make me afraid.

the people of Israel had not done so. And there was very great rejoicing. [18] And day by day, from the first day to the last day, he read from the Book of the Law of God. They kept the feast seven days, and on the eighth day there was a solemn assembly, according to the rule.

1. What happens during the feast of the seventh month?

2. What is the festival celebrating? (See Leviticus 23:33-43, especially v. 43.[17])

3. Why do they live in "booths"?

PONDER How does your reaction to the Word of God compare to that of the Israelites?

PRAYER IDEAS Ask God to make you thankful for and obedient to his Word.

READING 35   NEHEMIAH 9

Now on the twenty-fourth day of this month the people of Israel were assembled with fasting and in sackcloth, and with earth on their heads. [2] And the Israelites separated themselves from all foreigners and stood and confessed their sins and the iniquities of their fathers. [3] And they stood up in their place and read from the Book of the Law of the LORD their God for a quarter of the day; for another quarter of it they made confession and worshiped the LORD their God. [4] On the stairs of the Levites stood Jeshua, Bani, Kadmiel, Shebaniah, Bunni, Sherebiah, Bani, and Chenani; and they cried with a loud voice to the LORD their God. [5] Then the Levites, Jeshua, Kadmiel, Bani, Hashabneiah, Sherebiah, Hodiah, Shebaniah, and Pethahiah, said, "Stand up and bless the LORD your God from everlasting to everlasting. Blessed be your glorious name, which is exalted above all blessing and praise.

[6] "You are the LORD, you alone. You have made heaven, the heaven of heavens, with all their host, the earth and all that is on it, the seas and all that are in them; and you preserve all of them; and the host of heaven worships you. [7] You are the LORD, the God

who chose Abram and brought him out of Ur of the Chaldeans and gave him the name Abraham. [8] You found his heart faithful before you, and made with him the covenant to give to his offspring the land of the Canaanite, the Hittite, the Amorite, the Perizzite, the Jebusite, and the Girgashite. And you have kept your promise, for you are righteous.

[9] "And you saw the affliction of our fathers in Egypt and heard their cry at the Red Sea, [10] and performed signs and wonders against Pharaoh and all his servants and all the people of his land, for you knew that they acted arrogantly against our fathers. And you made a name for yourself, as it is to this day. [11] And you divided the sea before them, so that they went through the midst of the sea on dry land, and you cast their pursuers into the depths, as a stone into mighty waters. [12] By a pillar of cloud you led them in the day, and by a pillar of fire in the night to light for them the way in which they should go. [13] You came down on Mount Sinai and spoke with them from heaven and gave them right rules and true laws, good statutes and commandments, [14] and you made known to them your holy Sabbath and commanded them

---

17. See the appendix, p. 75.

commandments and statutes and a law by Moses your servant. 15 You gave them bread from heaven for their hunger and brought water for them out of the rock for their thirst, and you told them to go in to possess the land that you had sworn to give them.

16 "But they and our fathers acted presumptuously and stiffened their neck and did not obey your commandments. 17 They refused to obey and were not mindful of the wonders that you performed among them, but they stiffened their neck and appointed a leader to return to their slavery in Egypt. But you are a God ready to forgive, gracious and merciful, slow to anger and abounding in steadfast love, and did not forsake them. 18 Even when they had made for themselves a golden calf and said, 'This is your God who brought you up out of Egypt,' and had committed great blasphemies, 19 you in your great mercies did not forsake them in the wilderness. The pillar of cloud to lead them in the way did not depart from them by day, nor the pillar of fire by night to light for them the way by which they should go. 20 You gave your good Spirit to instruct them and did not withhold your manna from their mouth and gave them water for their thirst. 21 Forty years you sustained them in the wilderness, and they lacked nothing. Their clothes did not wear out and their feet did not swell.

22 "And you gave them kingdoms and peoples and allotted to them every corner. So they took possession of the land of Sihon king of Heshbon and the land of Og king of Bashan. 23 You multiplied their children as the stars of heaven, and you brought them into the land that you had told their fathers to enter and possess. 24 So the descendants went in and possessed the land, and you subdued before them the inhabitants of the land, the Canaanites, and gave them into their hand, with their kings and the peoples of the land, that they might do with them as they would. 25 And they captured fortified cities and a rich land, and took possession of houses full of all good things, cisterns already hewn, vineyards, olive orchards and fruit trees in abundance. So they ate and were filled and became fat and delighted themselves in your great goodness.

26 "Nevertheless, they were disobedient and rebelled against you and cast your law behind their back and killed your prophets, who had warned them in order to turn them back to you, and they committed great blasphemies. 27 Therefore you gave them into the hand of their enemies, who made them suffer. And in the time of their suffering they cried out to you and you heard them from heaven, and according to your great mercies you gave them saviors who saved them from the hand of their enemies. 28 But after they had rest they did evil again before you, and you abandoned them to the hand of their enemies, so that they had dominion over them. Yet when they turned and cried to you, you heard from heaven, and many times you delivered them according to your mercies. 29 And you warned them in order to turn them back to your law. Yet they acted presumptuously and did not obey your commandments, but sinned against your rules, which if a person does them, he shall live by them, and turned a stubborn shoulder and stiffened their neck and would not obey. 30 Many years you bore with them and warned them by your Spirit through your prophets. Yet they would not give ear. Therefore you gave them into the hand of the peoples of the lands. 31 Nevertheless, in your great mercies you did not make an end of them or forsake them, for you are a gracious and merciful God.

32 "Now, therefore, our God, the great, the mighty, and the awesome God, who keeps covenant and steadfast love, let not all the hardship seem little to you that has come upon us, upon our kings, our princes, our priests, our prophets, our fathers, and all your people, since the time of the kings of Assyria until this day. 33 Yet you have been righteous in all that has come upon us, for

you have dealt faithfully and we have acted wickedly. 34 Our kings, our princes, our priests, and our fathers have not kept your law or paid attention to your commandments and your warnings that you gave them. 35 Even in their own kingdom, enjoying your great goodness that you gave them, and in the large and rich land that you set before them, they did not serve you or turn from their wicked works. 36 Behold, we are slaves this day; in the land that you gave to our fathers to enjoy its fruit and its good gifts, behold, we are slaves. 37 And its rich yield goes to the kings whom you have set over us because of our sins. They rule over our bodies and over our livestock as they please, and we are in great distress.

38 "Because of all this we make a firm covenant in writing; on the sealed document are the names of our princes, our Levites, and our priests."

1. Summarize the point of the Levites' sermon in one paragraph (verse 28 will help).

2. What marks of repentance do you see throughout the chapter?

3. Even when enjoying the blessings of the Promised Land, Israel returns to sin. How is the Christian experience of sin similar to that of Israel? How is it different?

PONDER God never gives up on his people, despite their repeated unfaithfulness to him. How can the knowledge of this help us to avoid sin?

PRAYER IDEAS Pray that you and your church will learn the lessons of Israel's repeated disobedience and lapses into sin.

POINTER Nehemiah and Ezra are nowhere on view in this chapter; the Levites are in their proper place of priestly rule.

READING 36   NEHEMIAH 9:38-10:39

"Because of all this we make a firm covenant in writing; on the sealed document are the names of our princes, our Levites, and our priests."

10:1 On the seals are the names of Nehemiah the governor, the son of Hacaliah, Zedekiah, 2 Seraiah, Azariah, Jeremiah, 3 Pashhur, Amariah, Malchijah, 4 Hattush, Shebaniah, Malluch, 5 Harim, Meremoth, Obadiah, 6 Daniel, Ginnethon, Baruch, 7 Meshullam, Abijah, Mijamin, 8 Maaziah, Bilgai, Shemaiah; these are the priests. 9 And the Levites: Jeshua the son of Azaniah, Binnui of the sons of Henadad, Kadmiel; 10 and their brothers, Shebaniah, Hodiah, Kelita, Pelaiah, Hanan, 11 Mica, Rehob, Hashabiah, 12 Zaccur, Sherebiah, Shebaniah, 13 Hodiah, Bani, Beninu. 14 The chiefs of the people: Parosh, Pahath-moab, Elam, Zattu, Bani, 15 Bunni, Azgad, Bebai, 16 Adonijah, Bigvai, Adin, 17 Ater, Hezekiah, Azzur, 18 Hodiah, Hashum, Bezai, 19 Hariph, Anathoth, Nebai, 20 Magpiash, Meshullam, Hezir, 21 Meshezabel, Zadok, Jaddua, 22 Pelatiah, Hanan, Anaiah, 23 Hoshea, Hananiah, Hasshub, 24 Hallohesh, Pilha, Shobek, 25 Rehum, Hashabnah, Maaseiah, 26 Ahiah, Hanan, Anan, 27 Malluch, Harim, Baanah.

28 The rest of the people, the priests, the Levites, the gatekeepers, the singers, the temple servants, and all who have separated

themselves from the peoples of the lands to the Law of God, their wives, their sons, their daughters, all who have knowledge and understanding, [29] join with their brothers, their nobles, and enter into a curse and an oath to walk in God's Law that was given by Moses the servant of God, and to observe and do all the commandments of the LORD our Lord and his rules and his statutes. [30] "We will not give our daughters to the peoples of the land or take their daughters for our sons. [31] And if the peoples of the land bring in goods or any grain on the Sabbath day to sell, we will not buy from them on the Sabbath or on a holy day. And we will forego the crops of the seventh year and the exaction of every debt.

[32] "We also take on ourselves the obligation to give yearly a third part of a shekel for the service of the house of our God: [33] for the showbread, the regular grain offering, the regular burnt offering, the Sabbaths, the new moons, the appointed feasts, the holy things, and the sin offerings to make atonement for Israel, and for all the work of the house of our God. [34] We, the priests, the Levites, and the people, have likewise cast lots for the wood offering, to bring it into the house of our God, according to our fathers' houses, at times appointed, year by year, to burn on the altar of the LORD our God, as it is written in the Law. [35] We obligate ourselves to bring the firstfruits of our ground and the firstfruits of all fruit of every tree, year by year, to the house of the LORD; [36] also to bring to the house of our God, to the priests who minister in the house of our God, the firstborn of our sons and of our cattle, as it is written in the Law, and the firstborn of our herds and of our flocks; [37] and to bring the first of our dough, and our contributions, the fruit of every tree, the wine and the oil, to the priests, to the chambers of the house of our God; and to bring to the Levites the tithes from our ground, for it is the Levites who collect the tithes in all our towns where we labor. [38] And the priest, the son of Aaron, shall be with the Levites when the Levites receive the tithes. And the Levites shall bring up the tithe of the tithes to the house of our God, to the chambers of the storehouse. [39] For the people of Israel and the sons of Levi shall bring the contribution of grain, wine, and oil to the chambers, where the vessels of the sanctuary are, as well as the priests who minister, and the gatekeepers and the singers. We will not neglect the house of our God."

1. *The people of Israel agree to keep the commandments of the Law—and they put it in writing! Remembering that they were still under the rule of the King of Persia, what did the average Israelite have to do before he could sign (v. 28)?*

2. *Make a note of the three specific changes that will be involved (v. 30, v. 31, vv. 32-39).*
   -
   -
   -

3. *Read Jesus' words in Luke 3:8.[18] How will we know whether Israel's repentance is genuine?*

PONDER How can Christians encourage each other to "bear fruits in keeping with repentance"?

PRAYER IDEAS Commit yourself to being faithful to the Lord in both word and deed.

---

18. "Bear fruits in keeping with repentance. And do not begin to say to yourselves, 'We have Abraham as our father.' For I tell you, God is able from these stones to raise up children for Abraham."

Now the leaders of the people lived in Jerusalem. And the rest of the people cast lots to bring one out of ten to live in Jerusalem the holy city, while nine out of ten remained in the other towns. ² And the people blessed all the men who willingly offered to live in Jerusalem.

³ These are the chiefs of the province who lived in Jerusalem; but in the towns of Judah everyone lived on his property in their towns: Israel, the priests, the Levites, the temple servants, and the descendants of Solomon's servants. ⁴ And in Jerusalem lived certain of the sons of Judah and of the sons of Benjamin. Of the sons of Judah: Athaiah the son of Uzziah, son of Zechariah, son of Amariah, son of Shephatiah, son of Mahalalel, of the sons of Perez; ⁵ and Maaseiah the son of Baruch, son of Col-hozeh, son of Hazaiah, son of Adaiah, son of Joiarib, son of Zechariah, son of the Shilonite. ⁶ All the sons of Perez who lived in Jerusalem were 468 valiant men.

⁷ And these are the sons of Benjamin: Sallu the son of Meshullam, son of Joed, son of Pedaiah, son of Kolaiah, son of Maaseiah, son of Ithiel, son of Jeshaiah, ⁸ and his brothers, men of valor, 928. ⁹ Joel the son of Zichri was their overseer; and Judah the son of Hassenuah was second over the city.

¹⁰ Of the priests: Jedaiah the son of Joiarib, Jachin, ¹¹ Seraiah the son of Hilkiah, son of Meshullam, son of Zadok, son of Meraioth, son of Ahitub, ruler of the house of God, ¹² and their brothers who did the work of the house, 822; and Adaiah the son of Jeroham, son of Pelaliah, son of Amzi, son of Zechariah, son of Pashhur, son of Malchijah, ¹³ and his brothers, heads of fathers' houses, 242; and Amashsai, the son of Azarel, son of Ahzai, son of Meshillemoth, son of Immer, ¹⁴ and their brothers, mighty men of valor, 128; their overseer was Zabdiel the son of Haggedolim.

¹⁵ And of the Levites: Shemaiah the son of Hasshub, son of Azrikam, son of Hashabiah, son of Bunni; ¹⁶ and Shabbethai and Jozabad, of the chiefs of the Levites, who were over the outside work of the house of God; ¹⁷ and Mattaniah the son of Mica, son of Zabdi, son of Asaph, who was the leader of the praise, who gave thanks, and Bakbukiah, the second among his brothers; and Abda the son of Shammua, son of Galal, son of Jeduthun. ¹⁸ All the Levites in the holy city were 284.

¹⁹ The gatekeepers, Akkub, Talmon and their brothers, who kept watch at the gates, were 172. ²⁰ And the rest of Israel, and of the priests and the Levites, were in all the towns of Judah, every one in his inheritance. ²¹ But the temple servants lived on Ophel; and Ziha and Gishpa were over the temple servants.

²² The overseer of the Levites in Jerusalem was Uzzi the son of Bani, son of Hashabiah, son of Mattaniah, son of Mica, of the sons of Asaph, the singers, over the work of the house of God. ²³ For there was a command from the king concerning them, and a fixed provision for the singers, as every day required. ²⁴ And Pethahiah the son of Meshezabel, of the sons of Zerah the son of Judah, was at the king's side in all matters concerning the people.

²⁵ And as for the villages, with their fields, some of the people of Judah lived in Kiriath-arba and its villages, and in Dibon and its villages, and in Jekabzeel and its villages, ²⁶ and in Jeshua and in Moladah and Beth-pelet, ²⁷ in Hazar-shual, in Beersheba and its villages, ²⁸ in Ziklag, in Meconah and its villages, ²⁹ in En-rimmon, in Zorah, in Jarmuth, ³⁰ Zanoah, Adullam, and their villages, Lachish and its fields, and Azekah and its villages. So they encamped from Beersheba to the valley of Hinnom. ³¹ The people of Benjamin also lived from Geba onward, at Michmash, Aija, Bethel and its villages, ³² Anathoth, Nob, Ananiah, ³³ Hazor, Ramah, Gittaim, ³⁴ Hadid, Zeboim, Neballat,

35 Lod, and Ono, the valley of craftsmen.
36 And certain divisions of the Levites in Judah were assigned to Benjamin.

12:1 These are the priests and the Levites who came up with Zerubbabel the son of Shealtiel, and Jeshua: Seraiah, Jeremiah, Ezra, 2 Amariah, Malluch, Hattush, 3 Shecaniah, Rehum, Meremoth, 4 Iddo, Ginnethoi, Abijah, 5 Mijamin, Maadiah, Bilgah, 6 Shemaiah, Joiarib, Jedaiah, 7 Sallu, Amok, Hilkiah, Jedaiah. These were the chiefs of the priests and of their brothers in the days of Jeshua.

8 And the Levites: Jeshua, Binnui, Kadmiel, Sherebiah, Judah, and Mattaniah, who with his brothers was in charge of the songs of thanksgiving. 9 And Bakbukiah and Unni and their brothers stood opposite them in the service. 10 And Jeshua was the father of Joiakim, Joiakim the father of Eliashib, Eliashib the father of Joiada, 11 Joiada the father of Jonathan, and Jonathan the father of Jaddua.

12 And in the days of Joiakim were priests, heads of fathers' houses: of Seraiah, Meraiah; of Jeremiah, Hananiah; 13 of Ezra, Meshullam; of Amariah, Jehohanan; 14 of Malluchi, Jonathan; of Shebaniah, Joseph; 15 of Harim, Adna; of Meraioth, Helkai; 16 of Iddo, Zechariah; of Ginnethon, Meshullam; 17 of Abijah, Zichri; of Miniamin, of Moadiah, Piltai; 18 of Bilgah, Shammua; of Shemaiah, Jehonathan; 19 of Joiarib, Mattenai; of Jedaiah, Uzzi; 20 of Sallai, Kallai; of Amok, Eber; 21 of Hilkiah, Hashabiah; of Jedaiah, Nethanel.

22 In the days of Eliashib, Joiada, Johanan, and Jaddua, the Levites were recorded as heads of fathers' houses; so too were the priests in the reign of Darius the Persian. 23 As for the sons of Levi, their heads of fathers' houses were written in the Book of the Chronicles until the days of Johanan the son of Eliashib. 24 And the chiefs of the Levites: Hashabiah, Sherebiah, and Jeshua the son of Kadmiel, with their brothers who stood opposite them, to praise and to give thanks, according to the commandment of David the man of God, watch by watch. 25 Mattaniah, Bakbukiah, Obadiah, Meshullam, Talmon, and Akkub were gatekeepers standing guard at the storehouses of the gates. 26 These were in the days of Joiakim the son of Jeshua son of Jozadak, and in the days of Nehemiah the governor and of Ezra, the priest and scribe.

1. The walls are finished, but Jerusalem is still virtually a ghost town (this was first mentioned in 7:4[19]). Most people prefer life in the surrounding villages. What does this suggest about them?

2. Why is it important for people to live in Jerusalem (11:6, 11:8, 11:14, 11:19)?

3. What attitude do people have to those who settle in the city (11:2)?

PONDER How willing are you to move outside your 'comfort zone' for God and his plans?

PRAYER IDEAS Pray that God will establish himself and his service as the first priority of our hearts and minds.

POINTER The lists of Jews span across many generations of returning exiles, pulling together God's people in a way that goes beyond history.

---

19. The city was wide and large, but the people within it were few, and no houses had been rebuilt.

And at the dedication of the wall of Jerusalem they sought the Levites in all their places, to bring them to Jerusalem to celebrate the dedication with gladness, with thanksgivings and with singing, with cymbals, harps, and lyres. 28 And the sons of the singers gathered together from the district surrounding Jerusalem and from the villages of the Netophathites; 29 also from Beth-gilgal and from the region of Geba and Azmaveth, for the singers had built for themselves villages around Jerusalem. 30 And the priests and the Levites purified themselves, and they purified the people and the gates and the wall.

31 Then I brought the leaders of Judah up onto the wall and appointed two great choirs that gave thanks. One went to the south on the wall to the Dung Gate. 32 And after them went Hoshaiah and half of the leaders of Judah, 33 and Azariah, Ezra, Meshullam, 34 Judah, Benjamin, Shemaiah, and Jeremiah, 35 and certain of the priests' sons with trumpets: Zechariah the son of Jonathan, son of Shemaiah, son of Mattaniah, son of Micaiah, son of Zaccur, son of Asaph; 36 and his relatives, Shemaiah, Azarel, Milalai, Gilalai, Maai, Nethanel, Judah, and Hanani, with the musical instruments of David the man of God. And Ezra the scribe went before them. 37 At the Fountain Gate they went up straight before them by the stairs of the city of David, at the ascent of the wall, above the house of David, to the Water Gate on the east.

38 The other choir of those who gave thanks went to the north, and I followed them with half of the people, on the wall, above the Tower of the Ovens, to the Broad Wall, 39 and above the Gate of Ephraim, and by the Gate of Yeshanah, and by the Fish Gate and the Tower of Hananel and the Tower of the Hundred, to the Sheep Gate; and they came to a halt at the Gate of the Guard. 40 So both choirs of those who gave thanks stood in the house of God, and I and half of the officials with me; 41 and the priests Eliakim, Maaseiah, Miniamin, Micaiah, Elioenai, Zechariah, and Hananiah, with trumpets; 42 and Maaseiah, Shemaiah, Eleazar, Uzzi, Jehohanan, Malchijah, Elam, and Ezer. And the singers sang with Jezrahiah as their leader. 43 And they offered great sacrifices that day and rejoiced, for God had made them rejoice with great joy; the women and children also rejoiced. And the joy of Jerusalem was heard far away.

44 On that day men were appointed over the storerooms, the contributions, the firstfruits, and the tithes, to gather into them the portions required by the Law for the priests and for the Levites according to the fields of the towns, for Judah rejoiced over the priests and the Levites who ministered. 45 And they performed the service of their God and the service of purification, as did the singers and the gatekeepers, according to the command of David and his son Solomon. 46 For long ago in the days of David and Asaph there were directors of the singers, and there were songs of praise and thanksgiving to God. 47 And all Israel in the days of Zerubbabel and in the days of Nehemiah gave the daily portions for the singers and the gatekeepers; and they set apart that which was for the Levites; and the Levites set apart that which was for the sons of Aaron.

1. *How would you describe the celebration as the finished wall is finally dedicated?*

2. *There is repeated mention of King David in chapter 12. Why do you think this might be?*

MATTHEW 8-16

NEHEMIAH

HEBREWS 8-13

3. Think back to the written promises the people made and sealed in chapter 10 (see Reading 36). From verses 44-47, do they seem to be keeping them?

PONDER Do we find joy in serving God and his people?

PRAYER IDEAS Ask God to let us know the joy of our salvation.

READING 39   NEHEMIAH 13

On that day they read from the Book of Moses in the hearing of the people. And in it was found written that no Ammonite or Moabite should ever enter the assembly of God, [2] for they did not meet the people of Israel with bread and water, but hired Balaam against them to curse them—yet our God turned the curse into a blessing. [3] As soon as the people heard the law, they separated from Israel all those of foreign descent.

[4] Now before this, Eliashib the priest, who was appointed over the chambers of the house of our God, and who was related to Tobiah, [5] prepared for Tobiah a large chamber where they had previously put the grain offering, the frankincense, the vessels, and the tithes of grain, wine, and oil, which were given by commandment to the Levites, singers, and gatekeepers, and the contributions for the priests. [6] While this was taking place, I was not in Jerusalem, for in the thirty-second year of Artaxerxes king of Babylon I went to the king. And after some time I asked leave of the king [7] and came to Jerusalem, and I then discovered the evil that Eliashib had done for Tobiah, preparing for him a chamber in the courts of the house of God. [8] And I was very angry, and I threw all the household furniture of Tobiah out of the chamber. [9] Then I gave orders, and they cleansed the chambers, and I brought back there the vessels of the house of God, with the grain offering and the frankincense.

[10] I also found out that the portions of the Levites had not been given to them, so that the Levites and the singers, who did the work, had fled each to his field. [11] So I confronted the officials and said, "Why is the house of God forsaken?" And I gathered them together and set them in their stations. [12] Then all Judah brought the tithe of the grain, wine, and oil into the storehouses. [13] And I appointed as treasurers over the storehouses Shelemiah the priest, Zadok the scribe, and Pedaiah of the Levites, and as their assistant Hanan the son of Zaccur, son of Mattaniah, for they were considered reliable, and their duty was to distribute to their brothers. [14] Remember me, O my God, concerning this, and do not wipe out my good deeds that I have done for the house of my God and for his service.

[15] In those days I saw in Judah people treading winepresses on the Sabbath, and bringing in heaps of grain and loading them on donkeys, and also wine, grapes, figs, and all kinds of loads, which they brought into Jerusalem on the Sabbath day. And I warned them on the day when they sold food. [16] Tyrians also, who lived in the city, brought in fish and all kinds of goods and sold them on the Sabbath to the people of Judah, in Jerusalem itself! [17] Then I confronted the nobles of Judah and said to them, "What is this evil thing that you are doing, profaning the Sabbath day? [18] Did not your fathers act in this way, and did not our God bring all this disaster on us and on this city? Now you are bringing more wrath on Israel by profaning the Sabbath."

[19] As soon as it began to grow dark at the gates of Jerusalem before the Sabbath, I commanded that the doors should be shut and gave orders that they should not be opened until after the Sabbath. And I stationed some of my servants at the gates, that no load might be brought in on the Sabbath day. [20] Then

the merchants and sellers of all kinds of wares lodged outside Jerusalem once or twice. [21] But I warned them and said to them, "Why do you lodge outside the wall? If you do so again, I will lay hands on you." From that time on they did not come on the Sabbath. [22] Then I commanded the Levites that they should purify themselves and come and guard the gates, to keep the Sabbath day holy. Remember this also in my favor, O my God, and spare me according to the greatness of your steadfast love.

[23] In those days also I saw the Jews who had married women of Ashdod, Ammon, and Moab. [24] And half of their children spoke the language of Ashdod, and they could not speak the language of Judah, but the language of each people. [25] And I confronted them and cursed them and beat some of them and pulled out their hair. And I made them take oath in the name of God, saying, "You shall not give your daughters to their sons, or take their daughters for your sons or for yourselves. [26] Did not Solomon king of Israel sin on account of such women? Among the many nations there was no king like him, and he was beloved by his God, and God made him king over all Israel. Nevertheless, foreign women made even him to sin. [27] Shall we then listen to you and do all this great evil and act treacherously against our God by marrying foreign women?"

[28] And one of the sons of Jehoiada, the son of Eliashib the high priest, was the son-in-law of Sanballat the Horonite. Therefore I chased him from me. [29] Remember them, O my God, because they have desecrated the priesthood and the covenant of the priesthood and the Levites.

[30] Thus I cleansed them from everything foreign, and I established the duties of the priests and Levites, each in his work; [31] and I provided for the wood offering at appointed times, and for the firstfruits.

Remember me, O my God, for good.

1. After 12 years in Jerusalem as Governor, Nehemiah pays a return visit to King Artaxerxes in Babylon (v. 6). What happens while he is away? Look back to Reading 36, question 2 to see what specifically has gone wrong (see vv. 10-11; 15-16; 23-24).

2. How does Nehemiah react to this sin (vv. 11, 17, 19, 21, 22, 25, 28, 30)? Summarize this reaction.

3. Is Nehemiah's plea for God to remember his deeds a prayer for acknowledgment, or for pardon?

PONDER How do you react to sin? Do you feel the same zeal for God that Nehemiah has? In what ways would it be appropriate/inappropriate to respond as Nehemiah does?

PRAYER IDEAS Ask that God would teach you to see things his way, from his perspective, and to be horrified by sin as Nehemiah was.

READING 40   JEREMIAH 31:31-34; HEBREWS 8:6-13, 9:15

Jeremiah 31:31-34

"Behold, the days are coming, declares the LORD, when I will make a new covenant with the house of Israel and the house of Judah, [32] not like the covenant that I made with their fathers on the day when I took them by the hand to bring them out of the land of Egypt, my covenant that they broke,

though I was their husband, declares the Lord.
³³ But this is the covenant that I will make with the house of Israel after those days, declares the Lord: I will put my law within them, and I will write it on their hearts. And I will be their God, and they shall be my people. ³⁴ And no longer shall each one teach his neighbor and each his brother, saying, 'Know the Lord,' for they shall all know me, from the least of them to the greatest, declares the Lord. For I will forgive their iniquity, and I will remember their sin no more."

Hebrews 8:6-13

But as it is, Christ has obtained a ministry that is as much more excellent than the old as the covenant he mediates is better, since it is enacted on better promises. ⁷ For if that first covenant had been faultless, there would have been no occasion to look for a second.

⁸ For he finds fault with them when he says:

"Behold, the days are coming, declares the Lord,
   when I will establish a new covenant
      with the house of Israel
      and with the house of Judah,
⁹ not like the covenant that I made with
      their fathers
   on the day when I took them by the
      hand to bring them out of the
      land of Egypt.
For they did not continue in my covenant,
   and so I showed no concern for them,
      declares the Lord.
¹⁰ For this is the covenant that I will make
      with the house of Israel
   after those days, declares the Lord:
I will put my laws into their minds,
   and write them on their hearts,
and I will be their God,
   and they shall be my people.
¹¹ And they shall not teach, each one his
      neighbor
   and each one his brother, saying, 'Know
      the Lord,'
for they shall all know me,
   from the least of them to the greatest.
¹² For I will be merciful toward their
      iniquities,
   and I will remember their sins no more."

¹³ In speaking of a new covenant, he makes the first one obsolete. And what is becoming obsolete and growing old is ready to vanish away.

Hebrews 9:15

Therefore he is the mediator of a new covenant, so that those who are called may receive the promised eternal inheritance, since a death has occurred that redeems them from the transgressions committed under the first covenant.

1. The book of Hebrews takes up the issue of 'the problem with Israel.' What was wrong with the old covenant?

2. Hebrews 8:8-12 quotes Jeremiah 31:31-34. God had been planning a new covenant for a long time. How will it differ from the old one?

3. How is the new covenant enacted (Heb 9:15)?

PONDER God was incredibly patient with Israel. Why did he persevere (Jer 31:3)?

PRAYER IDEAS Thank God that in Christ's death, he remembers our sins no longer (Heb 8:12).

HEBREWS 8-13

INTRODUCTION

These readings are from the second half of the letter to the Hebrews. If you've done the studies in the third volume of *The Daily Reading Bible* you'll have read Hebrews 1-7, learning that in Jesus we have a covenant with God that goes beyond what was established by law. In Christ, we have a great high priest always interceding for us. In Hebrews 8-13, we will gain a deeper understanding of what Christ's death achieved. We will also be encouraged to persevere in the faith, to struggle with sin, and to devote ourselves to serving our fellow believers.

Here's an opening prayer you might like to use before each of the next 20 studies:

Heavenly Father, God of Peace,
We praise you for the gospel of Jesus, who became sin for us that we might be washed clean and considered holy in your sight. Strengthen our faith; we are tempted by sin, by hardship, and by bitterness and division. Enable us by your grace to overcome these trials, equip us to do your will, and lead us into holiness of life.
In Jesus' name,
Amen.

READING 41 — HEBREWS 8:1-2—LOOKING BACK

Now the point in what we are saying is this: we have such a high priest, one who is seated at the right hand of the throne of the Majesty in heaven, ² a minister in the holy places, in the true tent that the Lord set up, not man.

1. *"We have such a high priest …". The major theme of Hebrews 1-7 has been the person of Jesus, the Son, and his qualifications to be our high priest. Read over each of these passages from Hebrews 1-7, and try to sum up in one word or phrase the point being made about the Son and his priesthood in each passage.*

1:1-4
Long ago, at many times and in many ways, God spoke to our fathers by the prophets, ² but in these last days he has spoken to us by his Son, whom he appointed the heir of all things, through whom also he created the world. ³ He is the radiance of the glory of God and the exact imprint of his nature, and he upholds the universe by the word of his power. After making purification for sins, he sat down at the right hand of the Majesty on high, ⁴ having become as much superior to angels as the name he has inherited is more excellent than theirs.

2:14-18
Since therefore the children share in flesh and blood, he himself likewise partook of the same things, that through death he might destroy the one who has the power of death, that is, the devil, ¹⁵ and deliver

all those who through fear of death were subject to lifelong slavery. [16] For surely it is not angels that he helps, but he helps the offspring of Abraham. [17] Therefore he had to be made like his brothers in every respect, so that he might become a merciful and faithful high priest in the service of God, to make propitiation for the sins of the people. [18] For because he himself has suffered when tempted, he is able to help those who are being tempted.

4:14-16

Since then we have a great high priest who has passed through the heavens, Jesus, the Son of God, let us hold fast our confession. [15] For we do not have a high priest who is unable to sympathize with our weaknesses, but one who in every respect has been tempted as we are, yet without sin. [16] Let us then with confidence draw near to the throne of grace, that we may receive mercy and find grace to help in time of need.

7:23-26

The former priests were many in number, because they were prevented by death from continuing in office, [24] but he holds his priesthood permanently, because he continues forever. [25] Consequently, he is able to save to the uttermost those who draw near to God through him, since he always lives to make intercession for them.

[26] For it was indeed fitting that we should have such a high priest, holy, innocent, unstained, separated from sinners, and exalted above the heavens.

PONDER How does each of these attributes of Jesus make him the sort of high priest who is "fitting" for us and our needs (Heb 7:26)?

PRAYER IDEAS Thank God for each of these things that you've been reminded of about Jesus and his priesthood, and for the reasons why they are precious to you.

READING 42   HEBREWS 8:1-6—LOOKING FORWARD ■

Now the point in what we are saying is this: we have such a high priest, one who is seated at the right hand of the throne of the Majesty in heaven, [2] a minister in the holy places, in the true tent that the Lord set up, not man. [3] For every high priest is appointed to offer gifts and sacrifices; thus it is necessary for this priest also to have something to offer. [4] Now if he were on earth, he would not be a priest at all, since there are priests who offer gifts according to the law. [5] They serve a copy and shadow of the heavenly things. For when Moses was about to erect the tent, he was instructed by God, saying, "See that you make everything according to the pattern that was shown you on the mountain." [6] But as it is, Christ has obtained a ministry that is as much more excellent than the old as the covenant he mediates is better, since it is enacted on better promises.

1. What is the 'job description' of a priest?

2. The Israelite priests worked in a tent. Where did the design for this special tent come from?

3. This passage is a kind of introduction to the themes of the next three chapters, which are mainly about the superiority of Jesus and the new covenant. What's the basic reason given in this passage for why the new covenant is better than the old?

promises of God in Christ are you most grateful for?

PRAYER IDEAS Pray that God would give you a hunger to understand this part of his word, and that your times spent reading the Bible and praying over the next month would have a lasting effect on the way you think about God and relate to him.

PONDER Why would the new covenant promises be better than the old? What

---

READING 43   HEBREWS 8:6-13 ▢

But as it is, Christ has obtained a ministry that is as much more excellent than the old as the covenant he mediates is better, since it is enacted on better promises. ⁷ For if that first covenant had been faultless, there would have been no occasion to look for a second.

⁸ For he finds fault with them when he says:

"Behold, the days are coming, declares the Lord,
when I will establish a new covenant
    with the house of Israel
and with the house of Judah,
⁹ not like the covenant that I made with
    their fathers
on the day when I took them by the
    hand to bring them out of the
    land of Egypt.
For they did not continue in my covenant,
    and so I showed no concern for them,
    declares the Lord.
¹⁰ For this is the covenant that I will make
    with the house of Israel
after those days, declares the Lord:
I will put my laws into their minds,
    and write them on their hearts,
and I will be their God,
    and they shall be my people.
¹¹ And they shall not teach, each one his
    neighbor
    and each one his brother, saying, 'Know
        the Lord,'
for they shall all know me,

from the least of them to the greatest.
¹² For I will be merciful toward their
    iniquities,
    and I will remember their sins no more."

¹³ In speaking of a new covenant, he makes the first one obsolete. And what is becoming obsolete and growing old is ready to vanish away.

1. What are the differences between the new covenant and the old?

2. How are these differences connected with the fact that it is Jesus who is the mediator of this covenant?

PONDER Were there individuals within Israel who knew God and who experienced his forgiveness and the work of his Spirit before Jesus came? If so, what is new about the new covenant?

PRAYER IDEAS Give thanks to God for the forgiveness of your sins, for your knowledge of him and the desire in your heart to please him, that you have through the ministry of

Jesus. Think of several other fellow believers whom you are praying for today, and pray that you and they will have a deeper appreciation of these blessings.

READING 44 — HEBREWS 9:1-10

Now even the first covenant had regulations for worship and an earthly place of holiness. ² For a tent was prepared, the first section, in which were the lampstand and the table and the bread of the Presence. It is called the Holy Place. ³ Behind the second curtain was a second section called the Most Holy Place, ⁴ having the golden altar of incense and the ark of the covenant covered on all sides with gold, in which was a golden urn holding the manna, and Aaron's staff that budded, and the tablets of the covenant. ⁵ Above it were the cherubim of glory overshadowing the mercy seat. Of these things we cannot now speak in detail.

⁶ These preparations having thus been made, the priests go regularly into the first section, performing their ritual duties, ⁷ but into the second only the high priest goes, and he but once a year, and not without taking blood, which he offers for himself and for the unintentional sins of the people. ⁸ By this the Holy Spirit indicates that the way into the holy places is not yet opened as long as the first section is still standing ⁹ (which is symbolic for the present age). According to this arrangement, gifts and sacrifices are offered that cannot perfect the conscience of the worshiper, ¹⁰ but deal only with food and drink and various washings, regulations for the body imposed until the time of reformation.

1. *What meaning was communicated by each of the symbolic objects in the Most Holy Place of the tabernacle (vv. 3-5)?*

2. *What did 'worship' look like under the system of the Old Covenant?*

PONDER What do you think the worshipers in the tabernacle did with the guilty conscience that could never be cleared by their gifts and sacrifices?

PRAYER IDEAS Pray for the millions of people around the world enslaved to religious rituals with no knowledge of the steadfast love and compassion of God that are in Jesus.

POINTER The ESV translation of verses 8-9 reflects the fact that the same phrase is used in verses 2, 6 and 8 (translated variously in the NIV as "its first room", "the outer room" and "the first tabernacle"). Thus, the contrast in verses 8-9 is not between the Old Covenant era and the new, but between the present earthly age and the coming heavenly one: "By this the Holy Spirit indicates that the way into the holy places is not yet opened as long as the first section is still standing (which is symbolic for the present age)."

READING 45 — HEBREWS 9:11-22

But when Christ appeared as a high priest of the good things that have come, then through the greater and more perfect tent (not made with hands, that is, not of this creation) ¹² he entered once for all into the holy places, not by means of the blood of goats and calves but by means of his own blood, thus securing an eternal redemption. ¹³ For if the sprinkling of defiled persons with the blood of goats and bulls and with the ashes of a heifer sanctifies for the purification of the flesh, ¹⁴ how much more will the blood of Christ, who through the eternal Spirit offered himself without blemish to God, purify our conscience from dead works to serve the living God.

¹⁵ Therefore he is the mediator of a new covenant, so that those who are called may receive the promised eternal inheritance, since a death has occurred that redeems them from the transgressions committed under the first covenant. ¹⁶ For where a will is involved, the death of the one who made it must be established. ¹⁷ For a will takes effect only at death, since it is not in force as long as the one who made it is alive. ¹⁸ Therefore not even the first covenant was inaugurated without blood. ¹⁹ For when every commandment of the law had been declared by Moses to all the people, he took the blood of calves and goats, with water and scarlet wool and hyssop, and sprinkled both the book itself and all the people, ²⁰ saying, "This is the blood of the covenant that God commanded for you." ²¹ And in the same way he sprinkled with the blood both the tent and all the vessels used in worship. ²² Indeed, under the law almost everything is purified with blood, and without the shedding of blood there is no forgiveness of sins.

1. *What functions did the sprinkling of blood perform in the rituals of the Old Covenant (vv. 12, 13, 18-20, 21-22)?*

2. *How does the blood of Jesus fulfil all of these functions for us in the new covenant?*

PONDER What does it mean for us as new covenant people to "serve [worship] the living God" (v. 14)? What do you think it means for everything in that worship to be "sprinkled" by the blood of Jesus (cf. v. 21)?

PRAYER IDEAS Thank God for the way the blood of Jesus so thoroughly affects and pervades every aspect of our relationship with God and our service of him. Pray that we would understand that more clearly and live out that understanding in our feelings and words and actions.

READING 46   HEBREWS 9:23-28

Thus it was necessary for the copies of the heavenly things to be purified with these rites, but the heavenly things themselves with better sacrifices than these. ²⁴ For Christ has entered, not into holy places made with hands, which are copies of the true things, but into heaven itself, now to appear in the presence of God on our behalf. ²⁵ Nor was it to offer himself repeatedly, as the high priest enters the holy places every year with blood not his own, ²⁶ for then he would have had to suffer repeatedly since the foundation of the world. But as it is, he has appeared once for all at the end of the ages to put away sin by the sacrifice of himself. ²⁷ And just as it is

appointed for man to die once, and after that comes judgment, ²⁸ so Christ, having been offered once to bear the sins of many, will appear a second time, not to deal with sin but to save those who are eagerly waiting for him.

1. *What is the true 'place of holiness' that is the fulfilment of the symbolic tabernacle of the Old Covenant? What does it mean for us that Jesus has entered that place?*

2. What is the image we are supposed to have
   in our minds of what it means to 'wait'
   for Jesus' return (v. 28–cf. Lev 9:22-24[20])? as a weekly activity that happens in the
'sanctuary' of the church building? What are
some of the dangers of that mentality? What
part can you play in reforming those
practices and understandings?

PONDER Are there any remnants in your
own thinking or your church's practice of
the kind of understanding that sees 'worship'

PRAYER IDEAS Spend some time thinking
about what it will be like when Jesus returns
to consummate our salvation, and thanking
God for all that he has won for us.

READING 47   HEBREWS 10:1-10

For since the law has but a shadow of the
good things to come instead of the true
form of these realities, it can never, by the
same sacrifices that are continually offered
every year, make perfect those who draw
near. [2] Otherwise, would they not have ceased
to be offered, since the worshipers, having
once been cleansed, would no longer have
any consciousness of sin? [3] But in these
sacrifices there is a reminder of sin every year.
[4] For it is impossible for the blood of bulls
and goats to take away sins.
   [5] Consequently, when Christ came into the
world, he said,

"Sacrifices and offerings you have not
          desired,
   but a body have you prepared for me;
[6] in burnt offerings and sin offerings
   you have taken no pleasure.
[7] Then I said, 'Behold, I have come to do
          your will, O God,
   as it is written of me in the scroll of the
          book.'"

[8] When he said above, "You have neither
desired nor taken pleasure in sacrifices and
offerings and burnt offerings and sin

offerings" (these are offered according to the
law), [9] then he added, "Behold, I have come to
do your will." He abolishes the first in order
to establish the second. [10] And by that will we
have been sanctified through the offering of
the body of Jesus Christ once for all.

1. How did the sacrifices work as a "reminder
   of sin every year"?

2. What is the point being made by David in
   the verses quoted from Psalm 40? What
   did 'doing the Lord's will' mean for him?
   What did it mean for Jesus (cf. Isa 53:10[21])?

PONDER In how many ways was Jesus'
sacrifice different from the animal sacrifices
of the Old Covenant?

PRAYER IDEAS Thank God for the depth of
his love for you—that for your sake it was his
will to crush his own Son and see him suffer.

---

20. Then Aaron lifted up his hands toward the people and
blessed them, and he came down from offering the sin
offering and the burnt offering and the peace offerings.
[23] And Moses and Aaron went into the tent of meeting, and
when they came out they blessed the people, and the glory of
the LORD appeared to all the people. [24] And fire came out from
before the LORD and consumed the burnt offering and the

pieces of fat on the altar, and when all the people saw it, they
shouted and fell on their faces.
21. Yet it was the will of the LORD to crush him;
   he has put him to grief;
when his soul makes an offering for sin,
   he shall see his offspring; he shall prolong his days;
the will of the LORD shall prosper in his hand.

And every priest stands daily at his service, offering repeatedly the same sacrifices, which can never take away sins. ¹² But when Christ had offered for all time a single sacrifice for sins, he sat down at the right hand of God, ¹³ waiting from that time until his enemies should be made a footstool for his feet. ¹⁴ For by a single offering he has perfected for all time those who are being sanctified.

¹⁵ And the Holy Spirit also bears witness to us; for after saying,

¹⁶ "This is the covenant that I will make
        with them
    after those days, declares the Lord:
I will put my laws on their hearts,
        and write them on their minds,"

¹⁷ then he adds,

"I will remember their sins and their lawless
        deeds no more."

¹⁸ Where there is forgiveness of these, there is no longer any offering for sin.

1. What are the effects of Jesus' death and resurrection for us, his people? For his enemies?

2. In what sense have we been "perfected for all time" by the death of Jesus? In what sense are we "being sanctified"?

PONDER Try to come up with a metaphor or an illustration for what it means for Jesus to have "perfected for all time those who are being sanctified".

PRAYER IDEAS Think of several non-Christian people who are dear to you and pray that they would find forgiveness in Jesus while there is still opportunity.

Therefore, brothers, since we have confidence to enter the holy places by the blood of Jesus, ²⁰ by the new and living way that he opened for us through the curtain, that is, through his flesh, ²¹ and since we have a great priest over the house of God, ²² let us draw near with a true heart in full assurance of faith, with our hearts sprinkled clean from an evil conscience and our bodies washed with pure water. ²³ Let us hold fast the confession of our hope without wavering, for he who promised is faithful. ²⁴ And let us consider how to stir up one another to love and good works, ²⁵ not neglecting to meet together, as is the habit

of some, but encouraging one another, and all the more as you see the Day drawing near.

1. What does it mean to "draw near with a true heart in full assurance of faith"? Try to rewrite the whole clause, putting each phrase into other words that unpack what you think is meant.

2. *How do our meetings and other interactions "stir up one another to love and good works" (v. 24)? Does "encouraging one another" (v. 25) mean exactly the same as spurring on toward love and good deeds, or are there other dimensions to encouragement as well?*

PONDER If the 'sanctuary' in chapter 9 is heaven, do you think that the "confidence to enter" in verse 19 is primarily a reference to the present (when we pray) or to the future (when Jesus returns, or when we die)? If it is the future, what implications does that have for the present (cf. vv. 22, 23, 25; also Heb 4:16[22])?

PRAYER IDEAS Thank God for the enormous privilege of access into his presence through Jesus' death. Pray for the effect that you have by your words and your life on your fellow-believers, that you will be a spur and an encouragement.

POINTER "Bodies washed with pure water" in verse 22 is probably not a direct reference to baptism; more likely, "hearts sprinkled" and "bodies washed" are both metaphors, referring to the way Jesus' death does for us what the ritual purifications did symbolically for the priests of the Old Covenant—it purifies us to come into God's presence.

READING 50   **HEBREWS 10:26-31**

For if we go on sinning deliberately after receiving the knowledge of the truth, there no longer remains a sacrifice for sins, [27] but a fearful expectation of judgment, and a fury of fire that will consume the adversaries. [28] Anyone who has set aside the law of Moses dies without mercy on the evidence of two or three witnesses. [29] How much worse punishment, do you think, will be deserved by the one who has spurned the Son of God, and has profaned the blood of the covenant by which he was sanctified, and has outraged the Spirit of grace? [30] For we know him who said, "Vengeance is mine; I will repay." And again, "The Lord will judge his people." [31] It is a fearful thing to fall into the hands of the living God.

1. *How do verses 26-31 provide additional motivation and urgency to the*

instructions in verses 23-25?

2. *What reasoning does the writer use to respond to the idea that a person can have genuine, saving faith in Jesus that finds no expression in repentance and obedience?*

PONDER Do you think the writer is saying in these verses that you can be genuinely converted by God's spirit, and then fall away to eternal condemnation? Why/why not?

---

22. Let us then with confidence draw near to the throne of grace, that we may receive mercy and find grace to help in time of need.

READING 51   HEBREWS 11:1-16

Now faith is the assurance of things hoped for, the conviction of things not seen. ² For by it the people of old received their commendation. ³ By faith we understand that the universe was created by the word of God, so that what is seen was not made out of things that are visible.

⁴ By faith Abel offered to God a more acceptable sacrifice than Cain, through which he was commended as righteous, God commending him by accepting his gifts. And through his faith, though he died, he still speaks. ⁵ By faith Enoch was taken up so that he should not see death, and he was not found, because God had taken him. Now before he was taken he was commended as having pleased God. ⁶ And without faith it is impossible to please him, for whoever would draw near to God must believe that he exists and that he rewards those who seek him. ⁷ By faith Noah, being warned by God concerning events as yet unseen, in reverent fear constructed an ark for the saving of his household. By this he condemned the world and became an heir of the righteousness that comes by faith.

⁸ By faith Abraham obeyed when he was called to go out to a place that he was to receive as an inheritance. And he went out, not knowing where he was going. ⁹ By faith he went to live in the land of promise, as in a foreign land, living in tents with Isaac and Jacob, heirs with him of the same promise. ¹⁰ For he was looking forward to the city that has foundations, whose designer and builder is God. ¹¹ By faith Sarah herself received power to conceive, even when she was past the age, since she considered him faithful who had promised. ¹² Therefore from one man, and him as good as dead, were born descendants as many as the stars of heaven and as many as the innumerable grains of sand by the seashore.

¹³ These all died in faith, not having received the things promised, but having seen them and greeted them from afar, and having acknowledged that they were strangers and exiles on the earth. ¹⁴ For people who speak thus make it clear that they are seeking a homeland. ¹⁵ If they had been thinking of that land from which they had gone out, they would have had opportunity to return. ¹⁶ But as it is, they desire a better country, that is, a heavenly one. Therefore God is not ashamed to be called their God, for he has prepared for them a city.

1. *Why do you think the writer devotes a whole chapter to the theme of faith? How does it fit into the flow of the letter?*

2. *What do you think it means that "through his faith, though he died, [Abel] still speaks"? (Cf. Gen 4:10.[23])*

---

[23]. And the LORD said, "What have you done? The voice of your brother's blood is crying to me from the ground".

3. How do verses 13-16 sum up the main point that is being made by the examples quoted from Genesis?

PONDER Why do you think the words 'dead', 'died' and 'death' occur so many times in these verses?

PRAYER IDEAS Read verses 13-16 again and make them the basis for prayer for yourself and for the other Christians that you are praying for today. Ask God that this same sort of attitude would be yours, as you live in this world and wait for the next.

READING 52   HEBREWS 11:17-31

By faith Abraham, when he was tested, offered up Isaac, and he who had received the promises was in the act of offering up his only son, [18] of whom it was said, "Through Isaac shall your offspring be named." [19] He considered that God was able even to raise him from the dead, from which, figuratively speaking, he did receive him back. [20] By faith Isaac invoked future blessings on Jacob and Esau. [21] By faith Jacob, when dying, blessed each of the sons of Joseph, bowing in worship over the head of his staff. [22] By faith Joseph, at the end of his life, made mention of the exodus of the Israelites and gave directions concerning his bones.

[23] By faith Moses, when he was born, was hidden for three months by his parents, because they saw that the child was beautiful, and they were not afraid of the king's edict. [24] By faith Moses, when he was grown up, refused to be called the son of Pharaoh's daughter, [25] choosing rather to be mistreated with the people of God than to enjoy the fleeting pleasures of sin. [26] He considered the reproach of Christ greater wealth than the treasures of Egypt, for he was looking to the reward. [27] By faith he left Egypt, not being afraid of the anger of the king, for he endured as seeing him who is invisible. [28] By faith he kept the Passover and sprinkled the blood, so that the Destroyer of the firstborn might not touch them.

[29] By faith the people crossed the Red Sea as if on dry land, but the Egyptians, when they attempted to do the same, were drowned. [30] By faith the walls of Jericho fell down after they had been encircled for seven days. [31] By faith Rahab the prostitute did not perish with those who were disobedient, because she had given a friendly welcome to the spies.

1. How are the themes of verses 1-16 echoed in these verses?

2. How did faith in God's promises affect Moses' life and decision-making?

PONDER Part of the way that faith in God's promises shapes our lives is through obedience to God's direct commands. In what other ways does Moses' example suggest that faith in Jesus will make a difference to the choices we make in life?

PRAYER IDEAS Pray that God would give you the same spirit of faith as Moses, as you approach the choices and decisions of life.

And what more shall I say? For time would fail me to tell of Gideon, Barak, Samson, Jephthah, of David and Samuel and the prophets— 33 who through faith conquered kingdoms, enforced justice, obtained promises, stopped the mouths of lions, 34 quenched the power of fire, escaped the edge of the sword, were made strong out of weakness, became mighty in war, put foreign armies to flight. 35 Women received back their dead by resurrection. Some were tortured, refusing to accept release, so that they might rise again to a better life. 36 Others suffered mocking and flogging, and even chains and imprisonment. 37 They were stoned, they were sawn in two, they were killed with the sword. They went about in skins of sheep and goats, destitute, afflicted, mistreated— 38 of whom the world was not worthy—wandering about in deserts and mountains, and in dens and caves of the earth.

39 And all these, though commended through their faith, did not receive what was promised, 40 since God had provided something better for us, that apart from us they should not be made perfect.

1. How would you summarize the effect of faith in God and his promises upon the lives of the people referred to in these verses?

2. "All these ... did not receive what had been promised". What questions does Hebrews 11 raise regarding the faithfulness of God, and how does it answer them?

PONDER What light does Hebrews 11 shed on some of the popular misunderstandings and false teachings regarding faith that are common in churches today?

PRAYER IDEAS Pray for Christians today who are undergoing persecution and hardship for the sake of the name of Jesus. Ask God to strengthen their resolve to remain faithful, and give them a firm confidence in the resurrection. Try to find out some information about one particular country or congregation or situation where Christians are currently suffering such hardships, and make a commitment to pray regularly for them.

Therefore, since we are surrounded by so great a cloud of witnesses, let us also lay aside every weight, and sin which clings so closely, and let us run with endurance the race that is set before us, 2 looking to Jesus, the founder and perfecter of our faith, who for the joy that was set before him endured the cross, despising the shame, and is seated at the right hand of the throne of God.

3 Consider him who endured from sinners such hostility against himself, so that you may not grow weary or fainthearted. 4 In your struggle against sin you have not yet resisted to the point of shedding your blood. 5 And have you forgotten the exhortation that addresses you as sons?

"My son, do not regard lightly the
discipline of the Lord,
nor be weary when reproved by him.
6 For the Lord disciplines the one he loves,
and chastises every son whom he
receives."

7 It is for discipline that you have to endure. God is treating you as sons. For what son is there whom his father does not discipline? 8 If you are left without discipline, in which all have participated, then you are illegitimate children and not sons. 9 Besides this, we have had earthly fathers who disciplined us and we respected them. Shall we not much more be subject to the Father of spirits and live? 10 For they disciplined us for a short time as it seemed best to them, but he disciplines us for our good, that we may share his holiness. 11 For the moment all discipline seems painful rather than pleasant, but later it yields the peaceful fruit of righteousness to those who have been trained by it.

12 Therefore lift your drooping hands and strengthen your weak knees, 13 and make straight paths for your feet, so that what is lame may not be put out of joint but rather be healed.

1. In what ways does the writer want to encourage us to view the Christian life as a race? Which aspects of the metaphor apply?

2. What is the point that the writer is making about suffering and discipline in verses 4-13? How does it help us to view the hardships of the Christian life from that perspective?

PONDER In what sense do you think the word 'chastise' is used in verse 6?

PRAYER IDEAS Pray for Christian friends that you know who are currently undergoing sufferings and hardships; ask God to give them a thankful and submissive heart in the midst of their pain, and pray that the suffering would produce in them "the peaceful fruit of righteousness".

READING 55   HEBREWS 12:14-17

Strive for peace with everyone, and for the holiness without which no one will see the Lord. 15 See to it that no one fails to obtain the grace of God; that no "root of bitterness" springs up and causes trouble, and by it many become defiled; 16 that no one is sexually immoral or unholy like Esau, who sold his birthright for a single meal. 17 For you know that afterward, when he desired to inherit the blessing, he was rejected, for he found no chance to repent, though he sought it with tears.

1. What is meant by the "root of bitterness" in verse 15? (Cf. Deut 29:18-19.[24])

2. Why do you think sexual immorality is mentioned in this context?

3. Verse 13 urges us to strive for holiness. How is Esau an example of not striving for holiness?

PONDER How might the attitude of Esau show itself in your situation? Try to think of four or five examples of how it works out in practice.

---

24. "Beware lest there be among you a man or woman or clan or tribe whose heart is turning away today from the LORD our God to go and serve the gods of those nations. Beware lest there be among you a root bearing poisonous and bitter fruit, 19 one who, when he hears the words of this sworn covenant, blesses himself in his heart, saying, 'I shall be safe, though I walk in the stubbornness of my heart.' This will lead to the sweeping away of moist and dry alike."

PRAYER IDEAS Ask God to give you the kind of delight in him and in his promises that would massively outweigh the temptations of the world. Pray for friends who are currently in the grip of the sort of temptations referred to in these verses, that God would show them what it would cost them to walk away from Jesus.

READING 56   HEBREWS 12:18-29 ▪

For you have not come to what may be touched, a blazing fire and darkness and gloom and a tempest [19] and the sound of a trumpet and a voice whose words made the hearers beg that no further messages be spoken to them. [20] For they could not endure the order that was given, "If even a beast touches the mountain, it shall be stoned." [21] Indeed, so terrifying was the sight that Moses said, "I tremble with fear." [22] But you have come to Mount Zion and to the city of the living God, the heavenly Jerusalem, and to innumerable angels in festal gathering, [23] and to the assembly of the firstborn who are enrolled in heaven, and to God, the judge of all, and to the spirits of the righteous made perfect, [24] and to Jesus, the mediator of a new covenant, and to the sprinkled blood that speaks a better word than the blood of Abel.

[25] See that you do not refuse him who is speaking. For if they did not escape when they refused him who warned them on earth, much less will we escape if we reject him who warns from heaven. [26] At that time his voice shook the earth, but now he has promised, "Yet once more I will shake not only the earth but also the heavens." [27] This phrase, "Yet once more," indicates the removal of things that are shaken—that is, things that have been made—in order that the things that cannot be shaken may remain. [28] Therefore let us be grateful for receiving a kingdom that cannot be shaken, and thus let us offer to God acceptable worship, with reverence and awe, [29] for our God is a consuming fire.

1. What is the essential contrast between Mt Sinai and Mt Zion? How does that difference affect our relationship with God?

2. What similarities are still there between coming to Sinai and coming to Zion?

3. Read the prophecy in verse 26 from Haggai 2:6[25] in its original context. What is the place that is not shaken in Haggai? How does the writer to the Hebrews apply the verse here?

PONDER What was the word spoken by the blood of Abel? How does Jesus' blood speak a better word?

PRAYER IDEAS Thank God for the unshakeable kingdom that we look forward to on the basis of his promises, and for the assurance of salvation that we have through the blood of Jesus. Pray that God would give you the right mixture of confidence, joy and awe that goes with 'coming to Mt Zion'.

---

25. "'For thus says the LORD of hosts: Yet once more, in a little while, I will shake the heavens and the earth and the sea and the dry land. [7] And I will shake all nations, so that the treasures of all nations shall come in, and I will fill this house with glory, says the LORD of hosts. [8] The silver is mine, and the gold is mine, declares the LORD of hosts. [9] The latter glory of this house shall be greater than the former, says the LORD of hosts. And in this place I will give peace, declares the LORD of hosts.'"

Therefore let us be grateful for receiving a kingdom that cannot be shaken, and thus let us offer to God acceptable worship, with reverence and awe, 29 for our God is a consuming fire.

13:1 Let brotherly love continue. 2 Do not neglect to show hospitality to strangers, for thereby some have entertained angels unawares. 3 Remember those who are in prison, as though in prison with them, and those who are mistreated, since you also are in the body. 4 Let marriage be held in honor among all, and let the marriage bed be undefiled, for God will judge the sexually immoral and adulterous. 5 Keep your life free from love of money, and be content with what you have, for he has said, "I will never leave you nor forsake you." 6 So we can confidently say,

"The Lord is my helper;
   I will not fear;
what can man do to me?"

7 Remember your leaders, those who spoke to you the word of God. Consider the outcome of their way of life, and imitate their faith. 8 Jesus Christ is the same yesterday and today and forever. 9 Do not be led away by diverse and strange teachings, for it is good for the heart to be strengthened by grace, not by foods, which have not benefited those devoted to them. 10 We have an altar from which those who serve the tent have no right to eat. 11 For the bodies of those animals whose blood is brought into the holy places by the high priest as a sacrifice for sin are burned outside the camp. 12 So Jesus also suffered outside the gate in order to sanctify the people through his own blood. 13 Therefore let us go to him outside the camp and bear the reproach he endured. 14 For here we have no lasting city, but we seek the city that is to come. 15 Through him then let us continually offer up a sacrifice of praise to God, that is, the fruit of lips that acknowledge his name. 16 Do not neglect to do good and to share what you have, for such sacrifices are pleasing to God.

1. *Read the passage and jot down all the words and images to do with 'worship', 'sacrifices', 'altar', 'offerings', etc.*

2. *What sort of picture does chapter 13 paint of what it looks like to "offer to God acceptable worship"?*

PONDER Choose one of the verses in this passage (e.g. v. 2, v. 3, v. 5) and spend time thinking through what it would mean in practice for you to apply it in your situation.

PRAYER IDEAS Ask God to help you to put into practice the things that you have read in this passage; try to be specific in the kind of resolves that you are keen to ask for God's help in carrying out.

Let brotherly love continue. 2 Do not neglect to show hospitality to strangers, for thereby some have entertained angels unawares. 3 Remember those who are in prison, as though in prison with them, and those who are mistreated, since you also are in the body. 4 Let marriage be held in honor among all, and let the marriage bed be undefiled, for God will judge the sexually immoral and adulterous. 5 Keep your life free from love of money, and be content with what you have, for he has said, "I will never leave you nor forsake you." 6 So we can confidently say,

"The Lord is my helper;
    I will not fear;
what can man do to me?"

7 Remember your leaders, those who spoke to you the word of God. Consider the outcome of their way of life, and imitate their faith. 8 Jesus Christ is the same yesterday and today and forever.

1. Make a list of the commands in these verses.

2. Try to match the commands with the reasons that are given for them. How does each reason explain or motivate the command that it is attached to?

PONDER Repeat the exercise from Reading 57, this time with a different verse.

PRAYER IDEAS Once again, pray about your response to God's word, and for strength to put into practice the good resolves that God places on your heart. You might want to take the words of 2 Thessalonians 1:11-12 [26] and make them the basis of your prayer for yourself.

READING 59   HEBREWS 13:7-25

Remember your leaders, those who spoke to you the word of God. Consider the outcome of their way of life, and imitate their faith. 8 Jesus Christ is the same yesterday and today and forever. 9 Do not be led away by diverse and strange teachings, for it is good for the heart to be strengthened by grace, not by foods, which have not benefited those devoted to them. 10 We have an altar from which those who serve the tent have no right to eat. 11 For the bodies of those animals whose blood is brought into the holy places by the high priest as a sacrifice for sin are burned outside the camp. 12 So Jesus also suffered outside the gate in order to sanctify the people through his own blood. 13 Therefore let us go to him outside the camp and bear the reproach he endured. 14 For here we have no lasting city, but we seek the city that is to come. 15 Through him then let us continually offer up a sacrifice of praise to God, that is, the fruit of lips that acknowledge his name. 16 Do not neglect to do good and to share what you have, for such sacrifices are pleasing to God.

17 Obey your leaders and submit to them, for they are keeping watch over your souls, as those who will have to give an account. Let them do this with joy and not with groaning, for that would be of no advantage to you.

18 Pray for us, for we are sure that we have a clear conscience, desiring to act honorably in all things. 19 I urge you the more earnestly to do this in order that I may be restored to you the sooner.

20 Now may the God of peace who brought

---

26. To this end we always pray for you, that our God may make you worthy of his calling and may fulfill every resolve for good and every work of faith by his power, 12 so that the name of our Lord Jesus may be glorified in you, and you in him, according to the grace of our God and the Lord Jesus Christ.

again from the dead our Lord Jesus, the great shepherd of the sheep, by the blood of the eternal covenant, [21] equip you with everything good that you may do his will, working in us that which is pleasing in his sight, through Jesus Christ, to whom be glory forever and ever. Amen.

[22] I appeal to you, brothers, bear with my word of exhortation, for I have written to you briefly. [23] You should know that our brother Timothy has been released, with whom I shall see you if he comes soon. [24] Greet all your leaders and all the saints. Those who come from Italy send you greetings. [25] Grace be with all of you.

1. *What do we learn in these verses about the grace of God and the work of Christ?*

2. *How does grace 'strengthen our hearts'?*

PONDER What does it mean in practice to feed on God's grace? How can we make sure that our individual devotional life—and also the corporate meetings of the church that we belong to—has a 'diet' and a 'flavour' of grace?

PRAYER IDEAS Make a list of all that you have learned over the last month in Hebrews regarding God's grace and the work of God in Christ; make this list a basis for giving thanks to God for all you have in Jesus.

READING 60   HEBREWS 13:7-25 ▮

Remember your leaders, those who spoke to you the word of God. Consider the outcome of their way of life, and imitate their faith. [8] Jesus Christ is the same yesterday and today and forever. [9] Do not be led away by diverse and strange teachings, for it is good for the heart to be strengthened by grace, not by foods, which have not benefited those devoted to them. [10] We have an altar from which those who serve the tent have no right to eat. [11] For the bodies of those animals whose blood is brought into the holy places by the high priest as a sacrifice for sin are burned outside the camp. [12] So Jesus also suffered outside the gate in order to sanctify the people through his own blood. [13] Therefore let us go to him outside the camp and bear the reproach he endured. [14] For here we have no lasting city, but we seek the city that is to come. [15] Through him then let us continually offer up a sacrifice of praise to God, that is, the fruit of lips that acknowledge his name. [16] Do not neglect to do good and to share

what you have, for such sacrifices are pleasing to God.

[17] Obey your leaders and submit to them, for they are keeping watch over your souls, as those who will have to give an account. Let them do this with joy and not with groaning, for that would be of no advantage to you.

[18] Pray for us, for we are sure that we have a clear conscience, desiring to act honorably in all things. [19] I urge you the more earnestly to do this in order that I may be restored to you the sooner.

[20] Now may the God of peace who brought again from the dead our Lord Jesus, the great shepherd of the sheep, by the blood of the eternal covenant, [21] equip you with everything good that you may do his will, working in us that which is pleasing in his sight, through Jesus Christ, to whom be glory forever and ever. Amen.

[22] I appeal to you, brothers, bear with my word of exhortation, for I have written to

you briefly. [23] You should know that our brother Timothy has been released, with whom I shall see you if he comes soon. [24] Greet all your leaders and all the saints. Those who come from Italy send you greetings. [25] Grace be with all of you.

1. *Read back over the passage and list the ways that we are encouraged to respond to the grace of God and the work of Christ.*

2. *What role do our leaders play, according to these verses, in our feeding on and responding to the grace of God in Christ?*

PONDER What do you think it means for us to go "outside the camp" to Jesus?

PRAYER IDEAS Take the words of verse 20-21, and make them the basis for your prayers for yourself and for the fellow-believers whom you are praying for today.

MATTHEW 8-16

NEHEMIAH

HEBREWS 8-13

APPENDIX

ADDITIONAL PASSAGES REFERRED TO ...

Leviticus 13-14 (Reading 1)

The LORD spoke to Moses and Aaron, saying, [2] "When a person has on the skin of his body a swelling or an eruption or a spot, and it turns into a case of leprous disease on the skin of his body, then he shall be brought to Aaron the priest or to one of his sons the priests, [3] and the priest shall examine the diseased area on the skin of his body. And if the hair in the diseased area has turned white and the disease appears to be deeper than the skin of his body, it is a case of leprous disease. When the priest has examined him, he shall pronounce him unclean. [4] But if the spot is white in the skin of his body and appears no deeper than the skin, and the hair in it has not turned white, the priest shall shut up the diseased person for seven days. [5] And the priest shall examine him on the seventh day, and if in his eyes the disease is checked and the disease has not spread in the skin, then the priest shall shut him up for another seven days. [6] And the priest shall examine him again on the seventh day, and if the diseased area has faded and the disease has not spread in the skin, then the priest shall pronounce him clean; it is only an eruption. And he shall wash his clothes and be clean. [7] But if the eruption spreads in the skin, after he has shown himself to the priest for his cleansing, he shall appear again before the priest. [8] And the priest shall look, and if the eruption has spread in the skin, then the priest shall pronounce him unclean; it is a leprous disease.

[9] "When a man is afflicted with a leprous disease, he shall be brought to the priest, [10] and the priest shall look. And if there is a white swelling in the skin that has turned the hair white, and there is raw flesh in the swelling, [11] it is a chronic leprous disease in the skin of his body, and the priest shall pronounce him unclean. He shall not shut him up, for he is unclean. [12] And if the leprous disease breaks out in the skin, so that the leprous disease covers all the skin of the diseased person from head to foot, so far as the priest can see, [13] then the priest shall look, and if the leprous disease has covered all his body, he shall pronounce him clean of the disease; it has all turned white, and he is clean. [14] But when raw flesh appears on him, he shall be unclean. [15] And the priest shall examine the raw flesh and pronounce him unclean. Raw flesh is unclean, for it is a leprous disease. [16] But if the raw flesh recovers and turns white again, then he shall come to the priest, [17] and the priest shall examine him, and if the disease has turned white, then the priest shall pronounce the diseased person clean; he is clean.

[18] "If there is in the skin of one's body a boil and it heals, [19] and in the place of the boil there comes a white swelling or a reddish-white spot, then it shall be shown to the priest. [20] And the priest shall look, and if it appears deeper than the skin and its hair has turned white, then the priest shall pronounce him unclean. It is a case of leprous disease that has broken out in the boil. [21] But if the priest examines it and there is no white hair in it and it is not deeper than the skin, but has faded, then the priest shall shut him up seven days. [22] And if it spreads in the skin, then the

priest shall pronounce him unclean; it is a disease. 23 But if the spot remains in one place and does not spread, it is the scar of the boil, and the priest shall pronounce him clean.

24 "Or, when the body has a burn on its skin and the raw flesh of the burn becomes a spot, reddish-white or white, 25 the priest shall examine it, and if the hair in the spot has turned white and it appears deeper than the skin, then it is a leprous disease. It has broken out in the burn, and the priest shall pronounce him unclean; it is a case of leprous disease. 26 But if the priest examines it and there is no white hair in the spot and it is no deeper than the skin, but has faded, the priest shall shut him up seven days, 27 and the priest shall examine him the seventh day. If it is spreading in the skin, then the priest shall pronounce him unclean; it is a case of leprous disease. 28 But if the spot remains in one place and does not spread in the skin, but has faded, it is a swelling from the burn, and the priest shall pronounce him clean, for it is the scar of the burn.

29 "When a man or woman has a disease on the head or the beard, 30 the priest shall examine the disease. And if it appears deeper than the skin, and the hair in it is yellow and thin, then the priest shall pronounce him unclean. It is an itch, a leprous disease of the head or the beard. 31 And if the priest examines the itching disease and it appears no deeper than the skin and there is no black hair in it, then the priest shall shut up the person with the itching disease for seven days, 32 and on the seventh day the priest shall examine the disease. If the itch has not spread, and there is in it no yellow hair, and the itch appears to be no deeper than the skin, 33 then he shall shave himself, but the itch he shall not shave; and the priest shall shut up the person with the itching disease for another seven days. 34 And on the seventh day the priest shall examine the itch, and if the itch has not spread in the skin and it appears to be no deeper than the skin, then

the priest shall pronounce him clean. And he shall wash his clothes and be clean. 35 But if the itch spreads in the skin after his cleansing, 36 then the priest shall examine him, and if the itch has spread in the skin, the priest need not seek for the yellow hair; he is unclean. 37 But if in his eyes the itch is unchanged and black hair has grown in it, the itch is healed and he is clean, and the priest shall pronounce him clean.

38 "When a man or a woman has spots on the skin of the body, white spots, 39 the priest shall look, and if the spots on the skin of the body are of a dull white, it is leukoderma that has broken out in the skin; he is clean.

40 "If a man's hair falls out from his head, he is bald; he is clean. 41 And if a man's hair falls out from his forehead, he has baldness of the forehead; he is clean. 42 But if there is on the bald head or the bald forehead a reddish-white diseased area, it is a leprous disease breaking out on his bald head or his bald forehead. 43 Then the priest shall examine him, and if the diseased swelling is reddish-white on his bald head or on his bald forehead, like the appearance of leprous disease in the skin of the body, 44 he is a leprous man, he is unclean. The priest must pronounce him unclean; his disease is on his head.

45 "The leprous person who has the disease shall wear torn clothes and let the hair of his head hang loose, and he shall cover his upper lip and cry out, 'Unclean, unclean.' 46 He shall remain unclean as long as he has the disease. He is unclean. He shall live alone. His dwelling shall be outside the camp.

47 "When there is a case of leprous disease in a garment, whether a woolen or a linen garment, 48 in warp or woof of linen or wool, or in a skin or in anything made of skin, 49 if the disease is greenish or reddish in the garment, or in the skin or in the warp or the woof or in any article made of skin, it is a case of leprous disease, and it shall be shown to the priest. 50 And the priest shall examine the disease and shut up that which has the disease for seven days. 51 Then he shall

examine the disease on the seventh day. If the disease has spread in the garment, in the warp or the woof, or in the skin, whatever be the use of the skin, the disease is a persistent leprous disease; it is unclean. 52 And he shall burn the garment, or the warp or the woof, the wool or the linen, or any article made of skin that is diseased, for it is a persistent leprous disease. It shall be burned in the fire.

53 "And if the priest examines, and if the disease has not spread in the garment, in the warp or the woof or in any article made of skin, 54 then the priest shall command that they wash the thing in which is the disease, and he shall shut it up for another seven days. 55 And the priest shall examine the diseased thing after it has been washed. And if the appearance of the diseased area has not changed, though the disease has not spread, it is unclean. You shall burn it in the fire, whether the rot is on the back or on the front.

56 "But if the priest examines, and if the diseased area has faded after it has been washed, he shall tear it out of the garment or the skin or the warp or the woof. 57 Then if it appears again in the garment, in the warp or the woof, or in any article made of skin, it is spreading. You shall burn with fire whatever has the disease. 58 But the garment, or the warp or the woof, or any article made of skin from which the disease departs when you have washed it, shall then be washed a second time, and be clean."

59 This is the law for a case of leprous disease in a garment of wool or linen, either in the warp or the woof, or in any article made of skin, to determine whether it is clean or unclean.

14:1 The LORD spoke to Moses, saying, 2 "This shall be the law of the leprous person for the day of his cleansing. He shall be brought to the priest, 3 and the priest shall go out of the camp, and the priest shall look. Then, if the case of leprous disease is healed in the leprous person, 4 the priest shall command them to take for him who is to be cleansed two live clean birds and cedarwood and scarlet yarn and hyssop. 5 And the priest shall command them to kill one of the birds in an earthenware vessel over fresh water. 6 He shall take the live bird with the cedarwood and the scarlet yarn and the hyssop, and dip them and the live bird in the blood of the bird that was killed over the fresh water. 7 And he shall sprinkle it seven times on him who is to be cleansed of the leprous disease. Then he shall pronounce him clean and shall let the living bird go into the open field. 8 And he who is to be cleansed shall wash his clothes and shave off all his hair and bathe himself in water, and he shall be clean. And after that he may come into the camp, but live outside his tent seven days. 9 And on the seventh day he shall shave off all his hair from his head, his beard, and his eyebrows. He shall shave off all his hair, and then he shall wash his clothes and bathe his body in water, and he shall be clean.

10 "And on the eighth day he shall take two male lambs without blemish, and one ewe lamb a year old without blemish, and a grain offering of three tenths of an ephah of fine flour mixed with oil, and one log of oil. 11 And the priest who cleanses him shall set the man who is to be cleansed and these things before the LORD, at the entrance of the tent of meeting. 12 And the priest shall take one of the male lambs and offer it for a guilt offering, along with the log of oil, and wave them for a wave offering before the LORD. 13 And he shall kill the lamb in the place where they kill the sin offering and the burnt offering, in the place of the sanctuary. For the guilt offering, like the sin offering, belongs to the priest; it is most holy. 14 The priest shall take some of the blood of the guilt offering, and the priest shall put it on the lobe of the right ear of him who is to be cleansed and on the thumb of his right hand and on the big toe of his right foot. 15 Then the priest shall take some of the log of oil and pour it into the palm of his own left hand 16 and dip his right finger in the oil that is in his left hand and sprinkle some oil

with his finger seven times before the LORD. 17 And some of the oil that remains in his hand the priest shall put on the lobe of the right ear of him who is to be cleansed and on the thumb of his right hand and on the big toe of his right foot, on top of the blood of the guilt offering. 18 And the rest of the oil that is in the priest's hand he shall put on the head of him who is to be cleansed. Then the priest shall make atonement for him before the LORD. 19 The priest shall offer the sin offering, to make atonement for him who is to be cleansed from his uncleanness. And afterward he shall kill the burnt offering. 20 And the priest shall offer the burnt offering and the grain offering on the altar. Thus the priest shall make atonement for him, and he shall be clean.

21 "But if he is poor and cannot afford so much, then he shall take one male lamb for a guilt offering to be waved, to make atonement for him, and a tenth of an ephah of fine flour mixed with oil for a grain offering, and a log of oil; 22 also two turtledoves or two pigeons, whichever he can afford. The one shall be a sin offering and the other a burnt offering. 23 And on the eighth day he shall bring them for his cleansing to the priest, to the entrance of the tent of meeting, before the LORD. 24 And the priest shall take the lamb of the guilt offering and the log of oil, and the priest shall wave them for a wave offering before the LORD. 25 And he shall kill the lamb of the guilt offering. And the priest shall take some of the blood of the guilt offering and put it on the lobe of the right ear of him who is to be cleansed, and on the thumb of his right hand and on the big toe of his right foot. 26 And the priest shall pour some of the oil into the palm of his own left hand, 27 and shall sprinkle with his right finger some of the oil that is in his left hand seven times before the LORD. 28 And the priest shall put some of the oil that is in his hand on the lobe of the right ear of him who is to be cleansed and on the thumb of his right hand and on the

big toe of his right foot, in the place where the blood of the guilt offering was put. 29 And the rest of the oil that is in the priest's hand he shall put on the head of him who is to be cleansed, to make atonement for him before the LORD. 30 And he shall offer, of the turtledoves or pigeons, whichever he can afford, 31 one for a sin offering and the other for a burnt offering, along with a grain offering. And the priest shall make atonement before the LORD for him who is being cleansed. 32 This is the law for him in whom is a case of leprous disease, who cannot afford the offerings for his cleansing."

33 The LORD spoke to Moses and Aaron, saying, 34 "When you come into the land of Canaan, which I give you for a possession, and I put a case of leprous disease in a house in the land of your possession, 35 then he who owns the house shall come and tell the priest, 'There seems to me to be some case of disease in my house.' 36 Then the priest shall command that they empty the house before the priest goes to examine the disease, lest all that is in the house be declared unclean. And afterward the priest shall go in to see the house. 37 And he shall examine the disease. And if the disease is in the walls of the house with greenish or reddish spots, and if it appears to be deeper than the surface, 38 then the priest shall go out of the house to the door of the house and shut up the house seven days. 39 And the priest shall come again on the seventh day, and look. If the disease has spread in the walls of the house, 40 then the priest shall command that they take out the stones in which is the disease and throw them into an unclean place outside the city. 41 And he shall have the inside of the house scraped all around, and the plaster that they scrape off they shall pour out in an unclean place outside the city. 42 Then they shall take other stones and put them in the place of those stones, and he shall take other plaster and plaster the house.

43 "If the disease breaks out again in the house, after he has taken out the stones and

scraped the house and plastered it, ⁴⁴ then the priest shall go and look. And if the disease has spread in the house, it is a persistent leprous disease in the house; it is unclean. ⁴⁵ And he shall break down the house, its stones and timber and all the plaster of the house, and he shall carry them out of the city to an unclean place. ⁴⁶ Moreover, whoever enters the house while it is shut up shall be unclean until the evening, ⁴⁷ and whoever sleeps in the house shall wash his clothes, and whoever eats in the house shall wash his clothes.

⁴⁸ "But if the priest comes and looks, and if the disease has not spread in the house after the house was plastered, then the priest shall pronounce the house clean, for the disease is healed. ⁴⁹ And for the cleansing of the house he shall take two small birds, with cedarwood and scarlet yarn and hyssop, ⁵⁰ and shall kill one of the birds in an earthenware vessel over fresh water ⁵¹ and shall take the cedarwood and the hyssop and the scarlet yarn, along with the live bird, and dip them in the blood of the bird that was killed and in the fresh water and sprinkle the house seven times. ⁵² Thus he shall cleanse the house with the blood of the bird and with the fresh water and with the live bird and with the cedarwood and hyssop and scarlet yarn. ⁵³ And he shall let the live bird go out of the city into the open country. So he shall make atonement for the house, and it shall be clean."

⁵⁴ This is the law for any case of leprous disease: for an itch, ⁵⁵ for leprous disease in a garment or in a house, ⁵⁶ and for a swelling or an eruption or a spot, ⁵⁷ to show when it is unclean and when it is clean. This is the law for leprous disease.

Galatians 3:16–22 (Reading 27)

Now the promises were made to Abraham and to his offspring. It does not say, "And to offsprings," referring to many, but referring to one, "And to your offspring," who is Christ. ¹⁷ This is what I mean: the law, which came 430 years afterward, does not annul a covenant previously ratified by God, so as to make the promise void. ¹⁸ For if the inheritance comes by the law, it no longer comes by promise; but God gave it to Abraham by a promise.

¹⁹ Why then the law? It was added because of transgressions, until the offspring should come to whom the promise had been made, and it was put in place through angels by an intermediary. ²⁰ Now an intermediary implies more than one, but God is one.

²¹ Is the law then contrary to the promises of God? Certainly not! For if a law had been given that could give life, then righteousness would indeed be by the law. ²² But the Scripture imprisoned everything under sin, so that the promise by faith in Jesus Christ might be given to those who believe.

Romans 4:1–12 (Reading 27)

What then shall we say was gained by Abraham, our forefather according to the flesh? ² For if Abraham was justified by works, he has something to boast about, but not before God. ³ For what does the Scripture say? "Abraham believed God, and it was counted to him as righteousness." ⁴ Now to the one who works, his wages are not counted as a gift but as his due. ⁵ And to the one who does not work but trusts him who justifies the ungodly, his faith is counted as righteousness, ⁶ just as David also speaks of the blessing of the one to whom God counts righteousness apart from works:

⁷ "Blessed are those whose lawless deeds
    are forgiven,
  and whose sins are covered;
⁸ blessed is the man against whom the Lord
    will not count his sin."

⁹ Is this blessing then only for the circumcised, or also for the uncircumcised? We say that faith was counted to Abraham as righteousness. ¹⁰ How then was it counted to him? Was it before or after he had been circumcised? It was not after, but before he

was circumcised. [11] He received the sign of circumcision as a seal of the righteousness that he had by faith while he was still uncircumcised. The purpose was to make him the father of all who believe without being circumcised, so that righteousness would be counted to them as well, [12] and to make him the father of the circumcised who are not merely circumcised but who also walk in the footsteps of the faith that our father Abraham had before he was circumcised.

Leviticus 23:33–43 (Reading 34)

And the LORD spoke to Moses, saying, [34] "Speak to the people of Israel, saying, On the fifteenth day of this seventh month and for seven days is the Feast of Booths to the LORD. [35] On the first day shall be a holy convocation; you shall not do any ordinary work. [36] For seven days you shall present food offerings to the LORD. On the eighth day you shall hold a holy convocation and present a food offering to the LORD. It is a solemn assembly; you shall not do any ordinary work. [37] "These are the appointed feasts of the LORD, which you shall proclaim as times of holy convocation, for presenting to the LORD food offerings, burnt offerings and grain offerings, sacrifices and drink offerings, each on its proper day, [38] besides the LORD's Sabbaths and besides your gifts and besides all your vow offerings and besides all your freewill offerings, which you give to the LORD.

[39] "On the fifteenth day of the seventh month, when you have gathered in the produce of the land, you shall celebrate the feast of the LORD seven days. On the first day shall be a solemn rest, and on the eighth day shall be a solemn rest. [40] And you shall take on the first day the fruit of splendid trees, branches of palm trees and boughs of leafy trees and willows of the brook, and you shall rejoice before the LORD your God seven days. [41] You shall celebrate it as a feast to the LORD for seven days in the year. It is a statute forever throughout your generations; you shall celebrate it in the seventh month. [42] You shall dwell in booths for seven days. All native Israelites shall dwell in booths, [43] that your generations may know that I made the people of Israel dwell in booths when I brought them out of the land of Egypt: I am the LORD your God."

NOTES (see p. 8)

- Scribes/Teachers of the law

- Crowds

- Pharisees

- Sinners

-

Matthias Media is a ministry team of like-minded, evangelical Christians working together to achieve a particular goal, as summarized in our mission statement:

To serve our Lord Jesus Christ, and the growth of his gospel in the world, by producing and delivering high quality, Bible-based resources.

It was in 1988 that we first started pursuing this mission together, and in God's kindness we now have more than 250 different ministry resources being distributed all over the world. These resources range from Bible studies and books through to training courses and audio sermons.

To find out more about our large range of very useful products, and to access samples and free downloads, visit our website:

www.matthiasmedia.com.au

How to buy our resources

1. Direct from us over the internet:
    – in the US: www.matthiasmedia.com
    – in Australia and the rest of the world: www.matthiasmedia.com.au

2. Direct from us by phone:
    – in the US: 1 866 407 4530
    – in Australia: 1800 814 360 (Sydney: 9663 1478)
    – international: +61-2-9663-1478

3. Through a range of outlets in various parts of the world. Visit **www.matthiasmedia.com.au/international.php** for details about recommended retailers in your part of the world, including www.thegoodbook.co.uk in the United Kingdom.

4. Trade enquiries can be addressed to:
    – in the US: sales@matthiasmedia.com
    – in the UK: sales@ivpbooks.com
    – in Australia and the rest of the world: sales@matthiasmedia.com.au

MORE DAILY READINGS ...
VOLUMES 1-16 AVAILABLE

Volume 1

60 readings from
Matthew 5-6,
Joshua and
1 Corinthians 1-4.

Volume 2

60 readings from
1 Corinthians 5-7,
Malachi and
topical passages
about God's
trinitarian
characteristics..

Volume 3

55 readings from
Genesis 1-11,
2 Thessalonians,
Hebrews 1-7 and
topical passages
about Jesus.

Volume 4

60 readings from
Matthew 8-16,
Nehemiah and
Hebrews 8-13.

Volume 5

60 readings from
James, Genesis
12-35 and topical
passages about
the atonement.

Volume 6

60 readings from
Ephesians,
Lamentations and
Proverbs.

Volume 7

62 readings from
1 Peter, Zechariah,
Revelation 1-3 and
topical passages
about our present
suffering.

Volume 8

60 readings from
John 1-12,
Hosea and studies
on words.

Volume 9

60 readings from John 13-21, Isaiah 1-12 and Philippians.

Volume 10

60 readings from 1 Timothy, Exodus 1-18 and topical passages on 'the Christian calling'.

Volume 11

60 readings from 2 Peter, Genesis 36-50, Ecclesiastes and topical passages on the image of God.

Volume 12

60 readings from Elijah, Matthew 1-4 and 1 Thessalonians.

Volume 13

60 readings from Luke 1-6, Amos and 2 Corinthians.

Volume 14

60 readings from Luke 7-9, Micah and Galatians.

Volume 15

60 readings from Luke 9-15, Jonah and 2 Timothy.

Volume 16

62 readings from Luke 16-19, Job 1-26 and 1 Corinthians 8-16.

For more information or to order, contact:

Matthias Media
Telephone: +61-2-9663-1478
Facsimile: +61-2-9663-3265
Email: sales@matthiasmedia.com.au
www.matthiasmedia.com.au

Matthias Media (USA)
Ph: 1-866-407-4530
Fax: 724-964-8166
Email: sales@matthiasmedia.com
www.matthiasmedia.com

THE ESV BIBLE

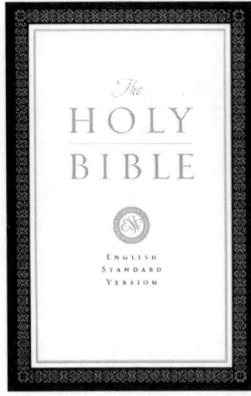

Since its much-anticipated release in late 2001, the English Standard Version (ESV) Bible has won increasing acceptance in churches throughout the US, England and Australia as an accurate, readable Bible for general use.

The secret of the ESV's success has been its ability to balance two crucial factors in Bible translation. On the one hand, it seeks to be an 'essentially literal' translation, retaining some of the form and flavour of the ancient text, and sticking as closely as possible to its thought-forms and imagery. At the same time, the ESV strives to be flowing and readable for a modern audience.

This balancing act is never possible to achieve perfectly, but the ESV is thought by many to do the best job of any English translation currently available.

This makes it suitable for a wide variety of purposes, including public reading and preaching, private and small group study, memorization, and so on.

"The English Standard Version is noticeably better than the currently most popular English translations of the Bible. The ESV brings us closer to what the authors actually wrote, and therefore what the Author actually says. Bible readers, teachers and preachers: this is the translation we have been waiting for, contemporary but more precisely accurate."

Rev. Dr John Woodhouse
Principal, Moore Theological College, Sydney

To find out more about the ESV, and to view online samples, go to

www.matthiasmedia.com.au/ESV